Kevi

CAMOUFLAGED
SISTERS
SILENT NO MORE!

Thank you for your service

L. Holley

" read from the front "

CAMOUFLAGED SISTERS
SILENT NO MORE!

LILA HOLLEY

& 11 Courageous Sisters in Arms

purposely
created
PUBLISHING

CAMOUFLAGED SISTERS

Published by Purposely Created Publishing Group™

Copyright © 2017 Lila Holley

ALL RIGHTS RESERVED.

Scriptures marked NIV are taken from the New International Version®. Copyright © 1973, 1978, 1984, 2011 by Biblica, Inc.™. All rights reserved.

Scriptures marked NKJV are taken from the New King James Version®. Copyright © 1982 by Thomas Nelson. All rights reserved.

Printed in the United States of America

ISBN: 978-1-945558-24-5

Special discounts are available on bulk quantity purchases by book clubs, associations and special interest groups. For details email: sales@publishyourgift.com or call (888) 949-6228.

For information logon to:
www.PublishYourGift.com

WHY THIS BOOK IS SO IMPORTANT

The timing is right for the release of Camouflaged Sisters: Silent No More. The authors of this book are courageous, and the sharing of their stories is necessary for their healing. My hope is that it brings to light the challenges that our sisters in arms face day in, day out, year in, year out. They are on the front line strategizing to take the fight to the enemy only to realize there are brothers and sisters in arms to their left, right, and behind them in the formation causing havoc. This book needs to be in the hands of every leader so they can read the firsthand knowledge of the pain these women have experienced and camouflaged for years. After reading this book you are now accountable for your actions and the actions of your subordinates. It is imperative that leaders foster a safe environment for our mothers, sisters, aunts, and grandmothers who serve in the armed forces. Lastly, I challenge you after reading this book to share it with others and encourage them to read it. Great work, ladies, I salute you!

Dylan Raymond
Chief Warrant Officer 3 (CW3), US Army Reserve
Author of *Rucksack to Briefcase*

It takes strength and courage to put pen to paper and write the not-so-pretty story of your life. The authors of Silent No More have done just that, with poise and dignity. The fact that these women chose to stand up and tell their stories has helped me to recognize that I do not stand alone in my experiences in life as well as in the military. My sisters have reminded me that despite the depth of the darkness, as long as I continue to STAND, the light will always shine!

Fatima Williams
SSgt (E-5), US Air Force Veteran

Silent No More, written by Lila Holley and the other eleven authors, provides readers a chance to step into the closed, often misunderstood world of military service for female military members. I found myself drawn to the cover, unable to remove my eyes from the masked, taped mouth. This symbol invoked within me memories of my own traumatic experiences. Thank you, ladies, for your strength and resiliency throughout your military service. Many will be blessed by this book.

Lucille Roane
Sergeant First Class (E-7), Retired US Army

Challenges that female military members face should not to be taken lightly. Though strong, they are sometimes taken advantage of physically, emotionally, and mentally. The women in Camouflaged Sisters: Silent No More exemplify courageous strength by sharing their struggles and providing healing for themselves and others.

Keisha Montague
First Sergeant (E-7), Retired US Air Force

Indeed, this work is a source of inspiration and encouragement for all women who are victims of sexual assault and domestic violence. The brave women here demonstrate true courage, resolve, and incredible strength in their personal spirit. It is my hope that as mothers, daughters, sisters, and fellow Veterans, we will share these powerful stories of survival and resilience.

Patricia Williams
Captain, US Army Veteran (1991–2002)

A powerful and eye-opening book from twelve women who bravely stand up and speak out about their experience in the military. Things that don't get talked about or pushed to the side, these sisters in arms come together and share what they have seen and gone through. The title speaks for itself—*Silent No More*. Read it!

Adam Bird
US Army Veteran

Faith is nothing more than one poor soul telling another where to find the bread of life. Throughout my military service, I felt isolated and unable to find peace as I navigated my way through the rough seas of adversity and conflict. But this book is now my "skiff" in high swells, and my ration of bread for spiritual survival as I weather the storms of adversity.

Tashandra Poullard-Houston
US Navy Veteran (1997–2006)

When I attended the book launch for *Camouflaged Sisters* in November 2015 with actor Miguel Nunez Jr., we listened as each coauthor shared her story of military service as an African American woman, discussing the challenges they faced during their careers. I thought that their stories were very interesting and could only imagine how difficult it must have been to face the struggles they went through. I'm very proud to see that Lila Holley is continuing to tell the stories of military women with

Silent No More. She continues to open our eyes to the challenges military women face day in and day out throughout their careers. Her books are to be added to the many resources available to our military sisters to help them cope with the challenges of a military career and to let them know that they are not alone in their journey. *Camouflaged Sisters: Silent No More* is a must read! To all my Camouflaged Sisters out there, I salute you all for your strength and courage to our country.

Renor Nori
Military Spouse

TABLE OF CONTENTS

TABLE OF CONTENTS CONTINUED

FOREWORD

There are many great themes in this life that will always bring a smile to the face of men and women alike, especially when it comes to our nation's armed forces. This theme affords great women of valor to take an oath and swear to defend the Constitution of the United States against all enemies, foreign and domestic. It is no doubt a very proud and boastful moment that will forever remain etched within the parameters of every Soldier, Sailor, Airman, and Marine.

What an awesome wonder to stand shoulder to shoulder with comrades without acknowledgment of color, gender, religion, or nationality, while sharing the common bond that bespoke of courage, strength, determination, discipline, honor, and loyalty to each other and those in need of protection. In the midst of that honorable moment in time, there are also unforeseeable forces, intrusions, which become permanent fixtures in the lives of these incredible military women in the form of sexual trauma, PTSD, depression, suicide, and domestic violence.

Camouflaged Sisters: Silent No More gives voice to the wounded and exposes the predator that continues to plague the minds of many victims who still suffer in silence.

FOREWORD

Such maladies possess the potential to render casualties powerless and defeated, as they become prisoners of an internal war. The dynamics addressed within this compilation of poignant events offer a measure of refuge and awareness. This insurmountable level of awareness serves as a unique tool designed to motivate readers to seek assistance in breaking the invisible chains of mental, emotional, and spiritual bondage. Through highlighting the stigmatism associated with mental illness, these courageous stories of survival offer tremendous support in the area of advocacy for victims of sexual assault, domestic violence, PTSD, depression, and suicide.

Silent No More is a beautiful anthology of strengths that binds us all together through our past, our uniform, our defeat, our pain, and our will to survive and triumph, as we transparently transition from victim to victor.

For my sisters in arms and many others like them, it is an absolute honor to read the journeys traveled by many but told by few!

Lolita R. Gilmore (MSG, Retired)
MS, LCDC
National Certified Victim Advocate
Teach Them To Love (T3L) Outreach Ministry

WE CANNOT REMAIN SILENT NO MORE...

Rape

Domestic Violence

Sexual Assault

Depression

Sexual Harassment

Post-Traumatic Stress Disorder

And the list goes on. This is the ugly part of our story as military women.

In this installment of Camouflaged Sisters, we take off the camouflage and reveal the ugly truth of our stories as women serving in uniform. This is a hard truth to share because it requires us to revisit the wrongdoing; the emotions; the smells, tastes, touches, and sounds of the memory of "that moment when . . ." A process we must go through to get to the good part of our story: the healing.

Writing this installment of Camouflaged Sisters has allowed us to dig deep and pull up courage we didn't know we possessed. Many of the authors in this book have never shared this part of their story with anyone before now. While some of the authors can't share enough, they are using their story to empower other sisters in arms to find the courage to move forward in their own healing process.

Sharing our stories of how we moved from trauma to triumph has allowed us to take back our power. We've changed the words we use to describe ourselves—we are no longer victims but survivors; we are no longer powerless but empowered; we have gone through trauma but have come out triumphant. We have rewritten our story—a story that must be told.

This journey has strengthened our bond of sisterhood. We are proud military women who have served our country honorably. We are leaders, planners, innovative thinkers, and go-getters. We are motivated, valued members of the team. We are Veterans. All titles we've earned. We embrace our titles and wear them proudly. Our story is not all good, and it is not all bad; however, it is a story worthy of sharing—every detail of it—the good, the bad, and the ugly.

Here is our story.

DOMESTIC VIOLENCE

Overcoming abuse doesn't just happen. It takes positive steps every day. Let today be the day you start to move forward.

—Assunta Harris

The following DoD directives govern how Commanders are to handle instances of domestic violence:

- *DoD Directive 1030.1 Victim and Witness Assistance (April 13, 2004)*
- *DoD Directive Family Advocacy Program 6400.1 (Aug 23, 2004)*
- *DoD Instruction Number 6400.06 Domestic Abuse Involving DoD Military and Certain Affiliated Personnel (August 21, 2007)*

1

You Deserve Peace

RAJSHEDA GRIFFIN

I Will Leave

"God, if you let me live, I promise I will leave this time."

This is all I could keep repeating to myself. I had once again been in a battle with my longtime boyfriend. When I say battle, I mean a scuffle that I did not participate in. He slung me across the room and suffocated me with a coat that he had tied around my head. I could feel my mind, soul, and spirit leaving me.

Did I mention I was about four-months pregnant?

As I collapsed to the floor, I heard the door slam. BOOM. Weak from the lack of oxygen, I could only muster enough strength to say and think that statement: *God, if you let me live,* I promise I will leave this time. As soon as I started to fade out, my boyfriend ran back into the house, untied the coat from around my head, and headed back to work. It took me about twenty minutes to regain my consciousness, and I was somewhat paralyzed from the lack of oxygen. I slowly moved toward the house phone and called my friend: "Come get me. I've had enough." She came to the house, and we made the great escape to my parents' home for safety.

This was my life at the young age of nineteen. I had been dating this man since the age of seventeen. He was six years older than I was and way more experienced. I fell in love quickly, and as soon as I was in love, and he knew it, the abuse began. Abuse is too nice of a word—let's call it his daily attempts to murder me. Throughout all I had experienced with him, I was still in love. With every beating came the comfort and the security of "I'm sorry," and "I will never do this again." Although it was never true, I kept hoping it would end.

It never did.

Abusers have a way of trapping women. They lure you with love, they seclude you from all who love and support you, they make you feel that you are nothing without them, and then they abuse you. You want help, but you believe that you cannot go to your loved ones because you cut everyone off for him. You feel bad for the abuser because he loves you so much. On top of that, you feel like you're nothing without him and that you will not survive because all you have is him. I fell into this trap over and over again. I finally realized that this was not love. I had another body living inside of me that needed me, and I had to survive.

Fast forward a few years, I had my beautiful child, and we were happy at my parents' house. I had found a part-time job and was looking into the idea of school. Right when I thought my life was coming together, the lion reared his head once more. After many attempts of trying to come back into my life, especially due to the pregnancy and the baby finally arriving, his main concern seemed to be wanting a family. So I packed my things and moved back in with him. The abusive man I knew had changed into a loving father and boyfriend again, but only for a short time. After a little over three months of living with him, the abuse started again. This time, he would use our child as a hostage. When I would try to leave, he would take her, and I couldn't fight him to get her back. It wasn't until a family friend decided to take her out for some ice cream that I gathered my things and left. I was done—tired of trying and tired of the abuse. My daughter was now involved, and this was not the loving home I wanted for her.

Being in this situation left me with high anxiety, insomnia, random flashbacks, and rolling panic attacks. Although I had all of these things going on, I needed to find a quick way to leave but still provide for me and my daughter. This is when I made the decision to join the US Army! Yes, the army. I could learn to fight, receive benefits, buy a home and a car, and have a stable career. This is exactly what I needed for me and my child! I could get away from him and all the issues. I soon realized that running away and not getting counseling was the wrong answer. When I entered Basic Training, I quickly found that the man I had wanted for so long to get away from was there in my face every day! No, he was not there physically, but I saw him in every Drill Sergeant, every Platoon Sergeant, and every leader who barked orders and yelled at the top of their lungs at me. My anxiety increased, but my realization that it was not my abuser made things somewhat manageable. It was, however, at this time that I realized this beast of abuse would follow me all the days of my life.

Flashbacks

Upon graduating Basic Training, I had a breath of fresh air—no more yelling—so there was relief. My anxiety calmed down, and things seemed to be leveling out. There were other incidents while serving, however, that made me feel like I was back in my hometown again, locked in a closet or trapped in a house.

We had military rollover drills one day. We all climbed inside a modeled Humvee that was built on a spinning machine. Once started, the machine would flip over and spin, first at a 180-degree turn to the right, then to the left, and then it would go for a barreling 360 spin. I began to panic a little because of the tight space of the Humvee, but I handled it well, knowing that this is what I had to do.

Then all of a sudden, without warning, the instructor stopped the rollover drill while we were mid-spin. This left us in an upside down position. The instructor hollered over the loud speaker, "Get out of the Humvee while it is upside down, and by the way, only one door opens!" At this point, I panicked. We unbuckled our seat belts and fell to the roof of the Humvee. There was a sea of bodies, and I was trapped!

"Hurry up! Someone find the unlocked door!" I hollered several times.

Everyone seemed to be moving in slow motion. *I then had a flashback of the suffocation incident.* I couldn't breathe, my hands became clammy, and I was sweating bullets. Then it happened—I freaked out. I started pushing people around, crying, and screaming, "help!" at the top of my lungs. Everything I couldn't say at the house I was being abused in, I said in that Humvee.

My battle buddies looked at me in disbelief. Someone finally hit the red panic button, and the instructor quickly came to my rescue. When I was outside in fresh air, I passed out. When I regained consciousness, everyone was staring at me and asking what happened. I had never been so embarrassed in my life. My past was haunting me, and until I chose to seek counseling, it would continue to haunt me. Running away to the protection of the army seemed like the right solution for me, but the different situations I encountered reminded me way too much of the issues of my past.

I loved my career, and I did not want to be chaptered (discharged) for having some form of PTSD, so I went on to seek counseling. I must admit that I did not want to at first. Counseling was for the weak, I thought, only the crazy people go there. I didn't want to be seen as someone who was weak and crazy. When I first started counseling, I was very shut down. I barely answered questions, and I was sick and tired of being asked if I was suicidal during every session (common protocol in VA counseling).

Then, I finally met the perfect counselor for me.

She had dealt with domestic abuse herself, and she knew just the right words to say and advice to give. It was amazing. I'm a praying woman, and I knew in my heart that God had sent her to me. After continual sessions with her, I slowly took control and took my life back. Although I still had issues with the military and the flashbacks, the techniques she taught me in those sessions helped me. I was able to continue my career successfully by accepting that the past was in the past, and that was where I needed to leave it.

Tell My Story

About five years down the line, I was stationed on the beautiful island of Okinawa, Japan. I enjoyed this place so much. There was no stress and no worries. No hard duties that reminded me of the past or caused me to have panic attacks or flashbacks. I was loving life. While stationed there, I worked as the Better Opportunity for Single Soldiers (BOSS) President. We had meetings on a regular basis, and each meeting, guest speakers told us about programs they provided and how they were there to help service members and families in need.

One day, we had a domestic violence advocate there. I must admit that when she first walked in, I rolled my eyes.

Not this again—I was not going to sit there and listen to this. I didn't want to hear the sad stories of abuse when I had long since gotten away from it. I quietly left the room and waited for her speech to be over. As I walked back in, she stopped me. "Why did you leave?"

"I had to use the restroom. I apologize," I lied.

She looked at me and said, "When you're ready to talk about your abuse, let me know."

I was in utter and complete shock. This woman I had never met before now just came up to me and said that. My immediate response was anger. I thought, *she can't talk to me like that!* There must be some kind of an interactive customer evaluation (ICE) complaint I can make against her! I'm the type of woman who lets things cool off before making rash decisions, so I let her say her piece before I went back to my barracks.

The next day, I decided that I would go to her office and speak to her about how she approached me. I went to the Army Community Service Building to find her. As I was walking by her office, I overheard a meeting about a ball that was coming up. They were discussing the Pink Dress Purple Tie Ball. (It was October, the month for breast cancer and domestic violence awareness.) They discussed all the guest speakers who would be attending.

I overheard her say that they currently had breast cancer survivors but no domestic violence survivors to speak at the ball. Everything in my gut wanted to volunteer, but I slowly turned and walked away. As I started to run off, here was the counselor in my face again. "I knew you would come to see me," she said.

As we sat there and talked, I finally unloaded my story about how I overcame my abusive past and how I had much more recovery to do. She expressed the need for a domestic violence survivor to speak at the upcoming ball. I was reluctant to do it, but I did.

The night had come for the Okinawa Pink Dress Purple Tie Ball, and I was extremely nervous. I had invited my whole chain of command and the BOSS program to support me. *It quickly hit me—I was about to expose myself! Everyone was going to know that I was abused!* I wanted to back out immediately. I went to speak to the counselor and told her that I was nervous and no longer wanted to do it. She assured me that this was a part of the healing process, and someone out there was being abused and needed to hear my words.

When the time came, my heels felt like they weighed a ton. I slowly walked to the podium. Everyone was looking at me: army officers and their spouses, my chain of command, and my Soldiers. "Well, here goes nothing,"

I said to myself. I took a deep breath and told my story. Before I knew it, tears were flowing from my eyes. This was the first time I had shared my story and spoke of the pain I had felt out loud! This was the first time I said the words *domestic violence survivor.* I was filled with emotions of hurt, anger, and regret; but I also felt relief, support, and love.

I looked out into the audience, and they were crying with me! They looked at me in support, not judgment. They all stood up, giving me a standing ovation. I was confused. I could not believe they were applauding me for sharing my story—my story of surviving domestic violence.

As I stepped down, Colonels came up to me and said they didn't check on their daughters as much as they should and that they would now. NCOs said they would be more aware of how they spoke to others because you never know what a person is going through. I had wives share that they were being abused and were scared to speak up, but they now had the courage to seek help. I was overwhelmed. All of this in the military!

This was my breaking point. This was what I needed to do. This was why I survived. I wanted to continue to share my story in hopes of helping those who were being abused find the courage to speak up. I hoped that my story would let them know that it was okay to cry, hurt, and regret. But more importantly, that it was okay to leave, seek help, and find yourself again.

As I started digging into my newfound passion, I discovered that there were quite a few holes in the system that is supposed to protect women who are abused on base. I also noticed that resources were somewhat limited. With my struggle and my triumph, I am currently in this fight for survivor protection and survivor assistance within the military. There are millions who aren't speaking up, and this is now my fight. My plea to the abused will always be, you did nothing wrong, you deserve happiness, you deserve peace, you deserve love, and you are worth it. I will continue this survivor fight because my past created my triumphant future for myself and for others!

2

You Deserve Help

Vivian Palmer

My Life

I could not believe this had become my life. I am a child of the Most High God. I am blessed and highly favored. I have been strategically assigned to a great purpose and destiny. I believe we all have a divine purpose for our lives. I believe that God works in us to guide and direct each one of us toward our divine goal and our destiny. I live by the scripture, "For I know the thoughts that I think toward you, says the Lord, thoughts of peace and not of evil, to give you a future and a hope" (Jeremiah 29:11 NKJV).

And while I knew all this to be true, I also knew that this had indeed become my life. I was an abused wife of a Soldier.

This is the first time I am writing these words in reference to myself. I admit it is extremely hard to do because I've grown used to living with this secret for so long. I know I must share my story, not only for my own growth and healing process but for other women who I know are in a similar situation. I must push past the shame, guilt, and embarrassment to tell my truth.

I come from a strong family with a military background and strong spiritual beliefs. I was born in Harlem, New York. My parents, Reverend Benjamin and Annie Palmer, ministers of the Gospel of Christ, raised me in the admonition of the Lord. Not only was I raised in the church, but my parents also prepared me for life—for as much as they knew, they poured it into me. The transitions I would eventually make in my life would require everything they taught me and more, especially in the military. I am immensely grateful and appreciative for their leadership and guidance. Their example of excellence has propelled me to a place of success within myself. I am truly blessed to have parents who took the time to impart into me their experience, wisdom, valuable insight, and knowledge, all of which have paved the way for me.

Not only are my parents great examples and leaders, but they are military Veterans (my father is a WWII Veteran). My parents were my biggest motivation to join the military. In addition to my parents, my siblings have proudly served: two brothers and two sisters, army, navy, and air force, respectively. In meticulously looking at my family and being the youngest daughter, I wanted to emulate my parents and siblings in their military careers. I am proud to be part of such a strong, powerful family that remains a great influence in my life, even today. My parents, who were high school sweethearts, have been married over sixty years and still serve the Lord, each other, and their family.

As a young girl, I can vividly remember the choir singing at my father's church, "I'm a Soldier in the army of the Lord." That was certainly my spiritual stance in my walk with God. As years have elapsed, my spiritual stance has transcended into the natural realm, and at twenty-one years old, I decided to follow my family by joining the US Army Healthcare Corps. It was there I learned to be a Soldier in the army for my country, the United States of America.

It's astounding how God prepares you in advance for what you will eventually walk in. All the lessons I had learned poised me for this very defining moment. My scriptural theme that has strengthened me time and time again has been, "You therefore, my son, be strong in the grace that is in Christ Jesus. And the things that you have heard of me among many witnesses, the same commit you to faithful men, who shall be able to teach others also. You therefore endure hardness, as a good soldier of Jesus Christ. No man that wars entangles himself with the affairs of this life; that he may please him who has chosen him to be a soldier" (2 Timothy 2:1-4 KJVER). This scripture has helped me tremendously, especially as it relates to leadership and exuding strength in the midst of struggle. I had to be strong and stand the test of time. My family and spiritual upbringing have helped me overcome a great deal of unexpected challenges.

Traveling the world was paramount for me. I desired greatly to see new things and experience various cultures and geographical locations. The military allotted me that opportunity, which I am thankful for. The military was most definitely an exciting experience. No longer did I have to listen to the military stories. I would develop my own stories and experiences. Today, I am blessed to be alive to write about them. All of my experiences, whether challenging or not, have shaped me to be the woman of virtue I am today. People see your glory on the surface, but they don't know your story. There was a price I had to pay to procure the current success and greatness of self I'm walking in today.

It started in Fort Jackson, South Carolina, where I attended Basic Training. There were many things about military life I was already accustomed to before my first day. What made things even smoother for me was my prior involvement in athletics. I was in great shape, very conditioned, and I understood the concept and principles of teamwork, character, hard work, and persistence. After Basic Training and successfully completing Advanced Individual Training (AIT), I went to my first permanent duty station. This was the turning point of my life.

Dark Days

I married a man I met in AIT, and on the surface, we had so much in common. We both were young and jumped right into marriage with no counseling. We moved forward in marriage because we just knew we loved each other and wanted to be together. Although I'd seen a great example of marriage through my parents, I wasn't properly equipped for my marriage covenant. Everything was based on impulsive, emotional feeling. I know now that my husband and I were unequally yoked, and the Bible I follow strictly warns against this, but I saw great qualities in this man.

In retrospect, I wish the military had pre-marital classes for new Soldiers wanting to wed. Most likely, that would have made a difference. If I had to give advice to a young couple who desired to marry while in the military, it would be, *seek wise counsel, submit to pre- and post-*

marital counseling, and sit down with your pastor. These are important prerequisites before marriage.

I believe everything happens for a divine purpose and reason. God makes no mistakes. And in the end, He causes all things to work together for the good. That's what God certainly did for me. However, going through this process and being a Soldier was extremely tough. After being married for a short period of time, the problems began, and it was a battle from the start to keep our marriage. During the roughest phase in our marriage, I was mentally, verbally, emotionally, and physically abused. My supervisor and his supervisor sent us to a mandatory meeting for military couples experiencing domestic violence. I equate the program to placing a Band-Aid on a broken leg. The daily meetings for a week did not work for us.

There were many times I tolerated the abuse due to fear of retaliation. You see, my husband was very popular in our military unit. I know now that this was not an adequate excuse, but it was mine at the time. Another piece of advice to all young couples going through any kind of abuse: *open your mouth and tell someone.* DO NOT *keep quiet.* No matter how much you want to protect your career or someone else's career in the military, it's just not worth it. I was extremely miserable and depressed. My perception of marriage was totally different than what I was experiencing. It left me in a very bad place. It was difficult having to go to work with all of this baggage and hurt, but I managed to put a smile on my face and pretend that everything was okay, which was extremely unhealthy for me.

Saving Grace

After birthing two beautiful children and transitioning into life as the military wife, I hid what was going on in my tumultuous household. This is a survival tool many spouses use in order to avoid negatively impacting our military spouse's career. My last and final straw was the feeling that death was inevitable. I feared I would not survive the outcome of the battle that was taking place in our home, so I finally reached out to his First Sergeant, who did not handle the problem appropriately and just swept it under the rug. It was apparent he was trying to protect my husband. *Domestic violence needs to be dealt with in a timely and efficient manner in every situation, but especially in a situation such as mine.*

The First Sergeant told me my husband could close quarters (terminate our housing agreement to live on post) and put us, his family, out, and there was nothing he could do for me. I could not believe this First Sergeant just told me my husband could put me and my children out in the streets, and he would not intervene. How could he condone this behavior? What he did not know was that I was former military, and I knew there was help for me on post. I was not going to settle for that response.

I dialed the Unit Commander's number—well, that was the number I thought I called—but before he even got his full name out, I stated with bold conviction, "If my body is found in the hospital morgue, just know I reached out for help!" I was in desperate need of help now! All I could think of as I stated those words was our last encounter and thinking, the next time, one of us will not make it out alive. Knowing that "someone" would likely be me, I knew I had to do something drastic. We had two small children, and all that was going through my mind was, if I die, who will raise my children? What a horrifying thought!

The man on the other side of the phone was not the Company Commander, but the Brigade (BDE) Commander. I truly believe God intervened and connected me to the top of the chain of command, as my previous attempts to get help from my spouse's immediate leadership ended with no results. He asked me a few questions, and I shared with him what had transpired and that the First Sergeant did not do anything about it. The BDE Commander said, "You don't have to worry, I will handle this matter. Please hold the line."

A few minutes later, he came back on the line and stated, "I have everyone I need on the line to go forward with what will take place from this moment on." The BDE Commander had the First Sergeant, the Company Commander, and my husband on the line and ordered them to stand at attention throughout the phone call. He was firm and straight to the point, requiring yes or no answers only. Then he asked my husband, "Do you wish to close quarters?"

My husband responded with, "Yes, sir," and the BDE Commander laid out the orders for them to follow and carry out immediately. Now, my husband had the financial responsibility to pay for us to live off post. I was very thankful for his leadership and quickness in handling a very serious matter. I will never forget how the BDE Commander showed excellent leadership that day. I've patterned my leadership to this day after him. I thank God for the BDE Commander—he was my angel! Thank you, sir! My phone call to you changed my life, and I am grateful.

Although we divorced, I still wanted the children to have a relationship with their father. No child should have to grow up without their father, so I made sure their relationship continued, just in separate households. The children were never in harm's way physically, but this was not a healthy environment for them to grow up in. We decided to be cordial and work together to give our children the absolute best. He has done a great job being actively involved in their lives. His love for his children was never in question, and that will never change. Our children are doing well, and our youngest recently graduated from college.

Despite all I've been through, I've been raised to walk in love and harbor forgiveness. These principles have helped me with my faith walk even more. My prayer life grew leaps and bounds. Taking each small step as a victory, I walked into one of my greatest victories, being the first African American woman Veteran in Central Texas to own a professional men's basketball team with the ABA, the Texas Sky Riders!

In closing, realize that your destiny shall not be denied. I would like to encourage everyone, especially wounded and abused women, that you can overcome it all. Your setback was nothing more than a setup for the greatest comeback in your life, despite all you've been through. Defeat and failure is not an option; only success, greatness, and destiny. If you have experienced hardship, pain, and failure, forgive yourself and forgive the offender. Don't live another day holding on to the past. Let it go, and shine bright as that precious jewel God created you to be. I truly believe there is greatness in us all. Keep the faith and believe in your dreams. As you release, you will position yourself to receive the greatest blessings of your life. It is your time, your turn, and your season. Now walk in it and be free.

3

You Deserve Life

Karen Wright-Chisolm

Never underestimate the power of someone else's struggles unless you have walked in their shoes.

The Struggle

I was seventeen years old, four-months pregnant, and two months away from graduating high school. I was scared to death that my parents, my teachers, and my friends would find out, and that I would not be allowed to graduate. I managed to conceal the truth until five months later, when I delivered my daughter on September 26, 1973. Little did I know that my life would change drastically from that day moving forward.

The man who I believed was the one I would spend the rest of my life became a living nightmare. We had been dating and living together for a while when the physical abuse started. Shortly before our daughter was

27

born, he joined the navy. We were separated for a while, but once he returned, we married. We were married for approximately one year when my son was born. I was excited, believing that a son would settle him down and force him to want to be a model father. I was wrong. His behavior did not change; if anything, it got worst. He began to take my son with him and expose him to acts of drugs and dealing with other women. There was always an argument whenever I would inquire about where he was or what he was doing.

For four years, I endured daily verbal and physical abuse. I never knew what to expect when he would come home from work. He was either high on drugs or drunk. I wanted to believe that he wanted to do better, but you guessed it—that never happened. There were times that I would get calls from the police department to come and pick up my children because their father had been taken to jail for shoplifting to support his habit or breaking and entering others' homes.

I worked shift work, so he was usually at home with the children at night. I finally realized that this was not the environment I wanted to raise my daughter or my son in. I was living a nightmare. I was afraid to be in the same house with him. Each time the abuse took place, I kept telling myself that he would change, and things would get better. *It never did.* I struggled for over nine years trying to sustain and take care of my two children. There were instances where the police were knocking at my door, children crying, and me being afraid to press charges or turn him in. It was very tough, but I kept trusting and believing that God would not put anymore on me than I could bear.

It was August 1, 1981, when God woke me up—not only from my restless night's sleep, but as it pertained to my life. This was the day that I would begin to transition from a life of domestic violence to a new beginning for me and my two children. I will never forget the words that God spoke to me as I sat up in my bed after my then husband left for work. God told me that *this was the time for me to escape from the tortures of my marriage—pack up and get out.*

I immediately jumped out of bed, made two phone calls, and began to pack up all of my possessions. I knew that I had to be packed and out of the house before he returned from work because if he knew what I was attempting to do, he would never let me leave there alive. I called my brother and a few of my friends, and we packed the house in less than seven hours. At approximately 2:45 p.m., we pulled away from the house, leaving only my husband's clothes in the bedroom closet, hanging all alone.

I wished I could have been a fly on the wall to see his expression as he turned the key to open the door, only to find that the house was empty, and we were gone. He made several attempts to contact me, but I knew that this was the only way I would be able to leave, and I refused to even entertain seeing him or answering his calls. He continued to attempt to contact me for about two weeks. In the past, I had left and returned over and over again, but I knew that this time, if I wanted to survive, I could not go back. After his failed attempts, I think he also realized that I was not giving in and coming back this time. This began my transition from a life of regular verbal and physical abuse to living and providing as a separated parent of two children.

After I got divorced, I decided that I needed to do something different with my life. I was afraid to get involved with anyone romantically for fear of having to relive the nightmares of the physical and verbal abuse that I had previously experienced. I was still working the job that required me to do shift work, which resulted in me spending lots of hours away from my children. I realized that this was not the lifestyle that I wanted to live, nor did I want to subject my children to it anymore. It was at this time that I began to get my body physically and mentally prepared to enter the United States Air Force Reserves.

The Struggle Continues

When I decided to join the military, I had been married and divorced, a single parent raising two children. I had been holding down a steady job, but I realized I wanted to do more with my life. I never imagined the experiences that I would have later in my life, the places I would travel, and the thousands of people I would meet.

Preparing my mind and body for what was about to become the beginning of the rest of my life was quite a process. It took me four years to situate my children and get my body in shape. I needed this time to regulate my mind to understand and believe that I could be someone different, and that the military would give me what I needed to take care of myself and my two children.

I entered the military at age thirty-one, but I knew that I had to do what I had to do. My children were separated from me again; however, I knew that it would only be temporary until I returned from Basic Training. My sisters were very supportive and took care of my children while I was gone.

It took me years to trust any man, and I continued to be paranoid about being close to a man. Because of the physical and sexual trauma that I experienced, I began to believe that this was natural. I began to wonder if

I was truly worthy of the respect that I desired. As I worked hard to make a better life for myself and my children, I found myself battling every day against men who tried to push me over the edge with verbal abuse, condescending emails, and daily questioning of my skills and knowledge. Every day, I had to prove myself worthy of success as an African American woman with credentials. This never-ending battle was exhausting—where and when would it end?

I now realize it may have seemed natural for me to marry a man that reminded me of my abusive father. For years, I experienced my dad coming home drunk and fighting my mother until he finally decided to leave. Even after they divorced, for years, I witnessed my mother drinking and engaging in relationships with men who were abusive, both physically and verbally.

The few memories from childhood and the history of my family have had a profound impact on the person I am today. I often ask myself, how is it that I only have bits and pieces of my childhood memories? I believe that the physical abuse that I witnessed for years as a child, growing up in a house where my father was abusive to my mother, caused me to block out memories of growing up. It was not until I began to write down my experiences that I was able to recall memories that were somehow blocked and placed in the back of my mind.

For years, I was mentally drained from continuing to let the memories of the physical and mental abuse slide until I decided that I would not and could not take it any longer. I was tired, and I had reached the end of my rope. I would have flashbacks of my father's friend cornering me in the house until I was finally able to get away; flashbacks of the countless times I had to hide and lock myself and my children in a closet, until my husband fell asleep, to protect us from his abusive rants. I endured flashbacks of my training instructor making sexual advances toward me as a way of intimidating me because of my age when I entered the military.

My decision to join the military was to escape my past of domestic violence and the dangers I felt at the time. Yes, I believed that my troubles were over and that I would finally be respected for the woman that I was. My defenses grew stronger as I attempted to prove myself worthy of more than physical, mental, and sexual abuse. Even though I faced challenges—instances of racial and sexual discrimination—I was able to overcome and make it through. I knew if I could overcome sexual trauma as a child and physical and verbal abuse in my marriage, I could overcome anything. Those experiences made me stronger and more determined to survive.

My Story Is Not Over

I've endured a lot in my life, and people close to me kept telling me, "You need to write a book." I listened, but I continued to put it off until I was reminded, time and time again, that *tomorrow is not promised.* You should never put off for tomorrow those things that you can and need to do now. I believe if I had not joined the military, I would not be as successful as I am today. The military taught me to overcome the many obstacles I endured and made me a better person. I was able to overcome and defeat the negative experiences of my life, determined not to be a statistic of violence but a statistic of success and endurance.

I turned my struggles into my success. I believe that God had a plan for my life, and if God had not freed me from my struggles, I would not be alive today to tell my story. People see me and think that I have always had it together, but they don't know my story. Had it not been for the prayers and support of my family, as well as the wisdom my grandmother and my mother passed on to me, I would have given up and given in a long time ago. I probably would not be alive today to tell my story.

I am in awe how God, in His own way, has renewed my spirit and prepared me for the things I need to do in order to move forward. The last ten years have been full of constant reminders of how important life is and that each of our lives has a purpose. Because of all the things I experienced in the most recent years of my life, I believe God's purpose for me will be revealed in the life experiences I share in this book.

It is my hope that someone can relate to the trials and tribulations that I have endured and realize that she too can overcome whatever obstacle she encounters in life. I hope that she believes that she can be successful in whatever she puts her mind to.

This little nappy-headed girl from "Back da Green," born with deformities of club feet, deprived of a normal life with both parents, raised primarily by her grandmother and grandfather, number "7 out of 11 plus 1" has finally found herself. I am proud to say I have made it through twenty-seven years and nine months of military service. I have achieved the highest rank that only 1 percent is able to attain, and I achieved the rank after a minimum of sixteen years in the military. I am a fast burner and a committed servant to my troops. I am well loved and respected by all I have met. While a single parent, I was able to complete an associate degree in personnel administration, a bachelor of science degree in human resources management, a dual master's degree in human resource management/development, and I am currently pursuing a doctorate of management degree in organizational leadership, culminating my career as the first black and first female Chief Master Sergeant to serve as the 315th Military Personnel Chief in the history of the organization at Charleston Air Force Base, South Carolina.

Before I put pen to paper, I pondered over what part of my story I would tell. I became overwhelmed at the many things I could write about. I have since married again and am happy in the life I have created for myself, but I believe that when you read the backstory of how I got here, you will have a greater appreciation and more respect for my journey. So many of us have incredible stories to tell, yet we believe that we cannot be successful because of where we come from, our past mistakes, and who we are as a result. Yes, the military played a major role in the person I am today compared to the person I was before I joined. For that I am forever grateful.

I am not really sure where these stories will lead me. I am not sure how many other lives will be impacted by my story, but what I know for sure is that God has put the vision in my heart and in my soul that I need to tell my story. It is my hope and my prayer that other sisters will be able to relate to my story and realize that they too can be successful. You see me, but can you see my struggles?

Order my steps for God's designated purpose.

We Are

Merci L. McKinley

We are not meant to live in defeat
Staying in a bottomless pit
Being tied to negative thoughts thinking we are weak
Standing still in choosing to quit

We are meant to move forward and live
Not thinking we are outcasts
We are meant to not just exist but to thrive
Not tied down to a past

We are meant to be exactly who we are
Embracing our uniqueness
Carrying a love for ourselves and never
letting it be too far
Leaping and bounding over hurdles
knowing possibilities are endless
We Are!

MILITARY SEXUAL TRAUMA

*My past has not defined me, destroyed me, deterred me,
or defeated me; it has only strengthened me.*

—Steve Maraboli

*Under DoD's confidentiality policy, sexual assault victims
are offered two reporting options: restricted reporting
and unrestricted reporting.*

RESTRICTED REPORTING

*Sexual assault victims who want to confidentially
disclose a sexual assault without triggering an official
investigation can contact a SARC/SHARP Specialist, VA/
SHARP Specialist, or a healthcare provider. By filing a
restricted report, a victim can disclose the sexual assault
without triggering an official investigation AND receive
medical treatment, advocacy services, legal assistance,
and counseling.*

UNRESTRICTED REPORTING

*This option is for victims of sexual assault who desire
medical treatment, counseling, legal assistance, SARC/
SHARP Specialist and VA/SHARP Specialist assistance, and
an official investigation of the crime. You will also be*

advised of your right to access to legal assistance that is separate from prosecution resources. At the victim's discretion/request, the healthcare provider shall conduct a sexual assault forensic examination (SAFE), which may include the collection of evidence.

(http://www.sexualassault.army.mil/)

4

You Will Make It

Merci L. McKinley

Soldier Through It

My name is Merci L. McKinley.

I had to constantly remind myself that as I struggled to reclaim who I was after my assaults. It is said that we all have a story within us, but how it is placed within is what gives it life. You never know if what you start will be a journey that stays with you for a lifetime. When I entered Basic Training, I had no idea what I was in for, but early on, it was a challenge that I was determined to adapt to and overcome. I arrived at Fort Leonard Wood, Missouri, as Private McKinley, but I had a difficult time passing the one-mile running requirement, which would allow me to advance. Immediately, I was shuttled in the cattle truck to a fitness-training unit for additional training so I could go on to Basic Training. I was given one more chance to show that I was not a failure.

The night before, I opened the Bible that my mother gave me as a gift for making straight As in the fourth grade. Little did I know, that would be the best gift given to me by anyone. I prayed to my heavenly Father to order my steps, as I didn't want to return home a failure. My mother always taught me to "trust in the Lord, lean not your own understanding and in all thy ways acknowledge Him and He shall direct your paths" (Proverbs 3:5-6). This scripture echoed in my mind as I opened my King James Version Bible, only to be led to Psalms 40:2 "He brought me up also out of a horrible pit, out of the miry clay, and set my feet upon a rock and established my goings." The next morning before my final Army Physical Fitness Training Test, I wrote this scripture on my running shoes. I went on to pass my fitness test. I would not be going home a failure.

Just five years after I completed Basic Training and started my career in the army, I realized how important that scripture would be in my life, as I would endure more than one sexual assault during the course of my military career. I had no idea how I was going to make it through. I didn't know if I was prepared to answer this challenge, or if I even had the ability to answer it.

In September of 2006, a newly assigned male Soldier sexually assaulted me. While I helped him in process, he showed interest in me, but I deflected his interest and made it perfectly clear that I did not want to engage in that with him. Months passed, he continued to ignore my wishes, and he forced himself on me while in the barracks. I was in complete shock. I could not believe this had happened to me. I felt even more violated when my case came back unfounded due to insufficient evidence because he wore a condom during the assault.

Months later, I prepared myself for reassignment to Germany and decided to email my old unit to inquire about my case. I contacted my former First Sergeant, whose reply was "to go on with your military career and put it behind you." I gave so much to my unit, especially while deployed, so I was once again shocked at the response. He stated, "More often than not, these cases come back unfounded, but do not let it define the rest of your career." I was in disbelief as I went through the embarrassment of a SANE (sexual assault nurse examiner) exam. *Why wasn't anyone other than me trying to hold this person accountable for what he did to me?* Nevertheless, I tried my best to "go on with my military career" and concentrate on my move to Germany.

In January 2007, I arrived in Baumholder, Germany, only to be faced with a second sexual assault by several male Soldiers in my new unit. During the assault, I was going in and out of consciousness, dazed and confused. Each time I came to, there was a different man on top of me.

At one point, I distinctly heard a knock on the door, and all I could do was gather my clothes, struggle to put them on, and get out of there as fast as I could.

After the assault, I immediately fled to my barracks room. My roommate was there, but she had no idea what was going on. I was crying and shaking and kept repeating, "I feel dirty, and I have to shower." At that point, she knew what had happened without me having to tell her. She went to get the Noncommissioned Officer (NCO) that was on Charge of Quarters (CQ) duty. They asked me if I had been assaulted, and I couldn't put into words what had happened because I was crying hysterically. I attempted to flee but fell down a flight of stairs. My roommate chased after me and held me close while the NCO notified the authorities.

I was transported to the hospital in Landstuhl, Germany, and was met by Criminal Investigation Division (CID) authorities. I underwent another SANE exam and had to disrobe while the nurse took pictures. When I was escorted back to my unit, the procedure was not to leave me alone. When I arrived to my Battalion Staff Duty, a victim advocate met me and informed me she had to go to battalion formation. I had to follow her although I was still in hospital scrubs. I didn't know anyone since I had just arrived in Germany, but everyone was pointing and whispering—they obviously knew me. I was paraded around as I shadowed this NCO. I was tired, still not showered, hungry, and in hospital scrubs. Even to this day, I still don't think she cared about what I was going through or that she was properly trained to respond in a situation like that.

The assault was classified as an "alcohol-related incident," so I was enrolled in the Army Substance Abuse Program. *I had to attend services at the very same location as my alleged perpetrators.* I had not yet earned my European driver's license and had to rely on others for transportation. Regardless, I knew I didn't want to receive services at the same location as those who assaulted me, so my attendance in counseling was sporadic at best. During this whole ordeal, I was alienated, and no one wanted to talk to me, like I was a disease. I begged my Command Sergeant Major (CSM) for a transfer, and he denied my request, telling me to "Soldier through it."

Eventually, I was transferred to another company in the same battalion, and I immediately began to spiral out of control. I turned to alcohol to cope with the trauma and violation. I was late to formations, utterly lost, and had not one friend I could honestly turn to. My former Platoon Sergeant asked me constantly if I wanted to be chaptered out of the army. He said, "I can get you chaptered out under a mental discharge." As I heard those words, I was falling apart inside. Just like in Basic Training, I did not want to go home a failure—you see, I wasn't just serving in the army for myself but for my siblings as well.

One day, I went back to my barracks room, and my roommate attempted to speak to me. She asked me what was wrong, and I screamed at her, "I'm tired, and I can't make it!" I went into the bathroom and locked myself inside. She started banging on the door, and the next voice I heard was that of my female First Sergeant.

She said, "McKinley, let me in. Open the door."

I sat there and prayed, "Lord, please help me. Father, I can't make it." I cried out, "Why? Answer me now please!" A voice told me to open the door and let my First Sergeant in. As she came in, I immediately collapsed in her arms.

I was completely broken.

I just started crying out, "I can't make it, First Sergeant!" I kept repeating this over and over. I even asked her for answers: *why did they do that to me?*

She showed me compassion as she held me close and said, "You can and you will make it." I pleaded with her to help me as I started shaking uncontrollably. First Sergeant comforted me and began to tell me about her female friend who was also a Soldier and had the same thing happen to her. I looked at her with tears in my eyes and asked, "Where is she now?"

"She is a First Sergeant now," she said softly, as she consoled me further.

Strength After Trauma

The next day, my First Sergeant enrolled me in another form of counseling, and I began to fight for my career. The investigation proceeded forward, and charges were officially filed. This time, there was *sufficient evidence,* and a male Soldier came forward and corroborated my story. He stated he had witnessed me going in and out of consciousness and two male Soldiers taking turns sexually assaulting me.

I felt vindicated, but when the trial came to hold the perpetrators accountable, I froze on the stand. No one on the legal team or in CID had put in the effort to prepare me for the witness stand. I had lost my voice as the Court Martial Convening Authority kept asking me, "Will you speak?" I looked at him and shook my head with a look in my eyes as if to say, "I can't find the words." I was immediately dismissed from the stand. The trial continued in my absence, as CID attempted to be my voice and testify on my behalf.

Days later, the Staff Judge Advocate General Office proposed a Chapter 10 for the defendants. They said there was enough evidence to show that this did happen to me, but because I lost my voice and didn't testify fully, this would be the only option for my assailants. *Army Regulation 635-200, Chapter 10, allows Soldiers to administratively separate in lieu of a court-martial by admitting to at least one charge, often times with an Other Than Honorable discharge.* This is a quick and expedient way to get rid of a service member pending UCMJ (Uniform Code of Military Justice) charges. I immediately signed the papers and left feeling defeated. I had never been without a voice before. I had never questioned who I was before.

I began the journey to "Soldier on" and threw myself into my work as an automated logistical specialist. This was my way of coping and putting the mission first. In time, I began to make friends who heard of my story but didn't come to pass judgment. I went on to reclaim my career, and months later, I won the Soldier of the Month Board and the other boards after that. I went on to attend the Warrior's Leaders Course in the middle of winter and graduated on the Commandant's List and as an honor graduate for my class. I deployed with my unit and received numerous awards and accolades for not only performing my duties well, but for the ability to adapt and overcome adversity. As I stood there knocking on the promotion board door, demanding and fighting for my advancement to the rank of Sergeant, *I was reminded of who I was in that moment.*

In 2009, during my promotion ceremony, I didn't want anyone else to pin me other than 1SG Melissa D. McFrazier, the First Sergeant who comforted me on that bathroom floor. As she stood before me to pin on my rank, she said, "You made it." I thought it was quite an honor for her to pin on my new rank, but she said she was the one who was honored to be pinning me.

I started out in Baumholder, Germany, broken beyond repair. I left renewed, knowing who I was with the rank of Sergeant. As I left, I looked toward the heavens above and knew that moment in the bathroom with now CSM McFrazier was similar to the moment I had when I decided to write Psalms 40:2 on my shoes in Basic Training. *I was brought up out of a pit and set upon a rock to establish my goings.*

In 2012, following my promotion to Staff Sergeant, I became a Sexual Harassment/Assault Response and Prevention (SHARP) victim advocate. I hit the ground running, as I noticed my battalion didn't have response kits. I thought back to the time in Germany when I was paraded around in hospital scrubs because there were no response kits. That memory of shame allowed me to reach down into my own pockets to purchase whatever I could to create female and male response kits. I assisted with writing the standard operating procedures (SOP) for victim advocates, determined to make the program better for future survivors. From the time I was a victim to eventually becoming a survivor, the SHARP program has improved by leaps and bounds, but there is still a long way to go.

When I took on my first case, I saw myself in a future survivor, as she sat there looking lost and in disbelief. I looked toward her just as my female First Sergeant did to me in Germany and said, "I know another person that this has happened to."

"What happened to that Soldier?" she asked me.

"She got the assistance she needed and became a Staff Sergeant."

She later asked for my assistance with a request to transfer from her unit, and I thought back to the time my Command Sergeant Major denied my request, and I had to walk around others who had disapproving looks. I went before her Chain of Command, became her voice, and saw her request through from start to finish. I made it my mission to help those in need to learn that there is strength after trauma, and they will become survivors through commitment to resilience. Resilience is not something you strive to put on as a show for others, but it is a gift you consciously choose to give yourself.

5

You Are Worthy

Cleve Williams

Deterioration of Trust

I went into training completely focused and determined to give my best in everything. The first incident occurred while in Basic Training as the company recruits returned to their bays from free time. A recruit began to make sexually suggestive comments to me about my rear end as he climbed the stairs behind me. I made it clear that I didn't like what he was saying and that I wanted him to stop. Another person even backed me up, telling him to stop. He laughed and grabbed my behind several times. I swiped at his hand to get him off of me and went to my Drill Sergeant.

I asked to use the "open-door policy" to see the First Sergeant (1SG). After explaining the incident to 1SG, he called our leaders into the office to discuss the matter. What occurred next was the beginning of the deterioration of my trust. The 1SG called me into the office and asked me to explain to my leaders and the other recruit's leaders what had happened. I held my head high and fought back tears as I recalled the incident again. I thought to myself, *how many times will I have to repeat this information?* They heard my complaint and asked me some questions, and the 1SG asked me to trust that the situation would be taken care of, and that paperwork on the incident would only cause me to look bad, causing a problem in my military career.

I asked if the situation was not serious enough to follow protocol. In that moment, a few tears escaped because I couldn't understand why the process for dealing with this type of situation was not being enforced or followed. I felt so angry and confused. As I stood there in silence, he reassured me that it would be dealt with and that the Platoon Sergeants would take care of it. The 1SG said that I wouldn't have to worry about coming in contact with the young man or seeing him anymore; then I was given a piece of tissue to clean my face. He told me to take as long as I needed to compose myself, and I could leave when I was ready. So I wiped my tears away and fanned my face with my hands to dry my eyes as I was escorted out by one of my Drill Sergeants. *That was only the beginning.*

Not Again

At my duty station, there was a young man who expressed interest in me. While passing through the hallway of the barracks one day, he asked me if I was in a relationship. I told him no and that I was not interested in a relationship because I was focusing on my career goals. He asked to take me on a date, and I declined, so we went our separate ways. Several months later, leading into one of our holiday breaks, a coworker asked me to hang out with her. She wanted to go to a party in the barracks, and we agreed to go together and leave together. That was very important to me because I didn't know as many people as she did. I knew her from training, so there was a level of trust already established.

As we entered the hall, we saw that the party was flowing through several rooms. Some were playing dominoes, and some were cooking food. I drank a wine cooler, we danced, and a few hours later, the party was slowing down for a movie. The room was still full of people, so everyone piled on the couch and on the floor. My battle buddy and I sat on the foot of the bed. My back was against the wall, and I ended up falling asleep there.

I awoke to see the man from the hall pulling my clothes off from the waist down. In my intoxicated state, I immediately looked for my buddy, but there was no one else in the room. The room was dark. I told him that I wanted to leave and to please let me get up. I pulled my clothes up to keep him from removing them, but he applied more force and continued to have his way. I cried for him to stop and told him that I was a virgin. I told him that I didn't want to have sex. He didn't stop. As he was trying to penetrate me, I screamed for help. I knew I was in real trouble when I noticed the guy in the room next door turn up the volume on his stereo to drown out my screams.

I tried to fight my way out of the situation. I felt like my mind was slowly slipping away from me as I looked into his empty eyes and wondered if I would survive. I felt like I was dying. Feeling completely helpless at this point, my mind started to wander. I thought about the guy next door and how he turned up the music to drown out my yells. I wondered why my battle buddy left me after we agreed to leave the party together. I wondered if I was going to die in this situation. I questioned, did my battle buddy intentionally bring me here for this to take place? Hopelessness settled in as I thought about how I should have stayed in my room instead of coming upstairs to this party.

As I tried to keep my mind off the assault taking place, I could hear my family telling me that this was my fault.

I could see their faces one by one. I could hear voices saying that God was disappointed in me and that He didn't love me. My last thought was, *how can I fix this?* I completely shut down as the tears continued to roll down my face, and I drifted further away. When he finished and rolled off of me, he instantly went to sleep. I quickly grabbed my clothes and walked out to return to my room. It seemed like it took me hours to get back to my room that night. I needed help. A few people saw me as they were returning to their rooms from a night of partying. Someone asked if I was all right. I wanted so badly to grab them and ask for their help, but the fear of them doing the same thing or ridiculing me kept me silent.

Once inside my room, I screamed and cried while cleaning myself. Afterward, I sat on the floor next to my bed crying. I screamed and cried so hard that eventually there was no sound, and my throat was sore for about a week. I cried myself to sleep, I cried when I woke up, and I cried myself back to sleep for days. I missed formations and work. I figured there was no point in showing up because I couldn't tell them what had happened. Why would I? So I could experience a repeat of what took place in Basic Training? To hear an NCO tell me how reporting this would "tarnish my military career and reputation"? I would not budge.

I wish I could tell you how long that ritual continued, but time seemed to stand still as complete shock set in. When I finally unlocked my doors, I was sent to the doctor because I wouldn't speak. The doctor wanted to do a full exam, and I screamed when he told me he would be doing a pelvic exam. I screamed and cried, so he didn't do the exam. He let me cry for a while and then released me to bed rest. I never said a word. I suffered in silence for months until I separated from the military.

I began counseling in a civilian office and was nurtured by my counselor, who expressed truly genuine love for me. My counselor was concerned about the choices I had made and was continuing to make as a result of what happened. I couldn't act on her counsel or believe it to be true for my life because I was paralyzed by fear.

From Fear to Freedom

I re-entered the military in August of 2000, and everything was so different for me. I truly wanted to complete the goals that I initially set for myself, and I was excited to be in a new place. Everything went very well for several months until the company went to the field, and I had a nightmare. During that time in service, I experienced panic attacks, blackouts, and depression. Life had become extremely stressful, and I could not pinpoint why everything felt so bad. The physical pain that resulted from anxiety and stress, accompanied with angry outbursts and destructive behavior, caused me to take a closer look at myself.

Not knowing the source of my physical pains led me to frequent sick call visits and various doctor appointments, which in turn led to questions and accusations of shamming. My NCOs did express concern and frustration about my absences from formations, tardiness to work, and my many appointments. I didn't feel like I could share the fullness of what I was dealing with just yet. Yes, it seemed like they genuinely cared, but my trust was diminished following that first incident in training and being let down by my NCOs then. I felt that keeping this information to myself was still necessary at the time.

I struggled with anger, depression, and destructive behaviors as I searched for the why behind my thoughts and actions. I removed everything in my possession that was not a necessity—televisions, game systems, movies, music—and everything that could distract me from taking the time to explore what was going on with me. I became very disconnected and forgetful, always misplacing things. I was very restless with pain in my neck and tension in my shoulders. My vision would blur at times, and I had constant headaches. As the physical pain continued to take its toll on me, I had become someone I didn't even recognize. I decided to enter in to counseling as a result. One day, the stress took its toll on me. I went to visit a friend with a coworker. I sat down in her room and told them about my headache. *Three days later*, I woke up in the hospital.

Throughout those years, I was able to identify a connection between the feelings I had about my trauma to my interactions with people at that time and the anxiety I was experiencing. I had lost hope and given up as a result of the assault against me. *This was enough to spark a new journey to heal completely from all of the trauma that I had disassociated from.*

It was time to cut the lock off of that secret shed and go through everything in it to release the past obstacles and live freely, not fearfully. I changed my mind about being hopeless and chose to live full of hope, forgiveness, love, and faith. That's when freedom came. Holding on to those negative emotions and the situations that promoted them only brought me to a worse state, both mentally and physically. To assist me with this healing process, I decided to go back into counseling. The three years when I did the most work to identify and change those behaviors were the years I experienced the most anxiety outside of the military. Deep breathing was a very effective tool for me to end the onset of a panic attack.

I also had great support at that time, which gave me the security I needed to continue the healing process. The unbearable became the key to enduring, and life became worth living once again. I soon developed a great and overwhelming love for everyone and everything. The joy that filled me was beyond measure. I am so thankful for the growth that came from my experience and the opportunity to help others who face similar challenges.

Over the years, I have volunteered my time and given love and care to people in difficult situations. In those times, I found myself telling them that I would not leave them to face the situation alone. *I know firsthand how important it is to seek the help needed for healing to overcome the effects of traumatic experiences.*

6

You Are Strong

Monique Jones

Comfortable

Courage is the invincible jeweled sword that cuts through all adversity. —Daisaku Ikeda

That is my mantra for today. Today, I confront a long-lived reality. Today, I stand in the courage reflecting back at me as I look in the mirror, releasing the realization of my truth. Today, I stand tall in the middle of the road, bare-skinned, without my camouflage. Today, I stand for *all* my sisters and brothers in arms who are still camouflaged in the scars and smoke of their stories, as I have been for many years.

In silence, we cover up with our smiles, we blend in with our fatigues and boots in formations, and we adapt to our surroundings. We burden in the choice to remain silent in exchange for our careers, our loved ones, and our children we must raise. We cry at night and lock away our pain in Pandora's box, knowing that if we speak our truth, the system may fail us in our goals for our future. Well, today is the first day of my future! *No longer in hiding, no longer in silence, and no longer in fear will I stay. Courage is my sword!*

"Jones, Jooonnsey! Girl, are you coming to the house tonight?" he asked. We were preparing to walk out the door and begin our holiday weekend after a long day in the operating room. My usual answer would be a no after such a long day, but I figured what the heck, why not? "Heeellloooo," he wakes me out of my contemplation. "Yes, Battle. Yes!" I responded boldly and sassy with a smile, "Sure, I'm in."

"For real? Don't bail as you always do."

"I promise, I will be there! See you all later!"

This was the exchange between myself and my trusted battle buddy that changed my life. These are the words that constantly replay and echo in my head. *This was the invite that would catapult my path into silence.*

Eight o'clock at night, I walked through the door of his condo to be greeted by the majority of the enlisted and sergeants in my unit. As I entered, I saw a few folks look at me strangely—guess they were surprised to see me there. I thought nothing of it because I usually did not go out or party with them. He saw me and smiled. "Hey girl, what you want to drink?"

"I'll take a light beer. I'm a lightweight," we all chuckled in agreement.

I sat down next to his wife and another female coworker, sipping on my beer, chatting, and sharing laughs. I thought to myself, *it is good to be social with my military family.* I had stopped hanging out after being drugged in a European nightclub a few years back. This was my first time out since that incident, and it felt good. I felt safer in the house-party, family-like setting versus a smoke-filled mega club.

One thing I noticed was that my battle buddy kept going into the bedroom with other people for a brief moment, and then they would come back out. I vaguely thought to myself, *that's odd.* Now that I look back, I wonder if this was intuition warning me.

I continued to mingle. Then my battle buddy's wife hugged me goodbye, explaining she was leaving to go babysit a friend's children. My battle walked her to the door, and as he returned, he asked if I wanted another drink. This time I refused because I knew I wanted to drive home in a little bit. He said, "Get comfy and enjoy yourself. Have one more, and if you feel you can't drive, you can crash in the extra room." Sounded reasonable to me, so I opted for another beer, knowing that was going to be my limit for the night.

Betrayal

As the night went on, I began to feel strange, like I was slightly sedated, and people were getting weird. They turned the lights out and started to play with neon chemical lights, Vick's vapor rub, and doctor face masks. As the lights swirled, déjà vu! I knew that I had been drugged, and my nightmare in Europe was replaying itself. How could I be so vulnerable to allow this to happen a second time? I was truly disappointed in those who took advantage of me, but more so in myself!

Ecstasy was a popular drug among club-goers and grew in use among the military while I was stationed in Europe. I did not think that it was still relevant many years later in the United States and, more importantly, among the troops.

I thought to myself, *how do I get out of here? I'm just going to have to ride it out.* Starting the internal panic, I had to get some fresh air. I stepped onto the balcony, and small hallucinations started to kick in. All I could do was sit on the ground, breathe in fresh air, and drink water while spiraling into a semi-trance. My female coworker came up to me and asked me how I was feeling and if I was rolling, a common term used for an ecstasy high. I just nodded at her with no words, thinking to myself, *how many people are in on this? How could I be so trusting? How could my battle buddy betray me?*

As the night lingered on, I felt worse. He spotted me and asked if I was okay. I responded with a "not so much," as he escorted me to his bathroom. He proceeded to run me a bath and provided me with some boxers and a white t-shirt. He then told me the bath would make me feel better, and he apologized for the drink. He explained he thought I knew, and that his wife had told him I wanted to try the ecstasy—that's why he crushed it into my drink. He rationalized his behavior with my clean reputation in the unit and not wanting any of the others see me go into the bathroom.

I couldn't believe I had gotten myself into this situation, and my so-called battle buddy's reasoning for trying to "save my good reputation" didn't relieve him of blame in this situation. By this point, I was completely helpless, as the drugs had taken full effect on me, and the bath had rendered my body limp. I told myself, I'm okay, in a very real state of high and delusion. This was unlike anything that I had ever felt before. I tried to fight it, but I fell asleep, or more like into unconsciousness.

I wasn't sure how much time had passed, but I woke up with him on top of me, in me, pumping on me. *My goodness, NO! Not this way!* I think that I am speaking. I swear I was screaming out loud, but no words managed to leave my lips. I fought and made attempts to get him—all 200 pounds of him—off me, but my efforts were futile. As I slipped in and out of consciousness during this whole ordeal, the hallucinations were magnified as I watched his face morph into that of a monster, just like the ones seen in vampire movies. After what seemed like an eternity, he finally finished and thanked me, saying this meant so much to him. I was numb, speechless, and in total shock.

He then escorted me through the living room to the guest bedroom as I heard a female voice faintly ask if I was okay. He responded, "She is okay—just having a bad trip." Sadly, of all the people at the party, all those from my unit, no one checked on me from that point on. The next day, I woke up on the floor with my original clothing lying next to me. I dressed and took a few moments to collect my thoughts. My mind began to race. *What would happen if I said something now? Okay, I'll tell the command, but who? Nearly everyone in the unit had attended the party!*

I went into the living room where he was sitting with his wife and a few others who stayed. He acted as if nothing ever happened, and she asked if I had fun. Did she know? I said nothing and made my way to use the bathroom. I avoided looking in the mirror. I just couldn't face myself as I processed the shame and feeling of knowing he raped me.

Silence

For the next two days, I recovered from being drugged, and I continued to contemplate if I would report what had happened. When I returned to work, a female coworker who was at the party asked me what had happened. She said she noticed he took me in his room, and she asked me if he had sex with me. While everything inside of me wanted to scream out the truth of that situation, I just couldn't tell her what had happened to me. I also wondered, was this her way of telling me the same thing had happened to her? I couldn't take any chances, and at that point, I decided to remain silent. Death to the truth, I declared!

I had way too much to lose: my rank, my newly promotable status, and my deployed fiancé who would be home in forty-two days for R&R leave. As I rationalized my decision in my mind, I concluded that "the system" was not truly set up for me as a victim. Once I admitted that drugs and drinking played a part in this assault, my character and the truthfulness of my story would be thrown into question. Not to mention the many people from the unit in attendance at this party where drugs were being consumed. It would turn into a their-word-against-mine battle, and the fact that I was sexually assaulted would be lost in the chaos. I chose not to be punished for speaking out; plus, the girls who made these kinds of reports were usually deemed as troublemakers or liars. At least that was what I saw, and I didn't want this label.

I was a good Soldier and wanted to keep it that way. I valued my career in uniform. I loved it so much that I was willing to simply shut up and continue to show up day after day as if nothing had ever happened. Sadly, I knew there was no way possible in those days to secretly seek help without it impacting my career in some way, so I chose my career over myself, becoming *camouflaged in my trauma.*

The choice I made allowed me to continue in the career and life in the military that I had grown to love. Do not think that this was an easy decision for me. I suffered greatly. I was in a total state of shock and went into recluse. I felt as if I did not know who I could trust. Naturally, I'm an energetic and vibrant person, so falling prey to betrayal of this magnitude was sheer shock to my system—it shocked my inner spirit. I stopped participating in all unit functions for the remainder of my time in that unit and never spoke with those in attendance of the party outside of work again.

As I share my story now, in my own words, for the first time publicly, I wonder how many others are like me, suffering in silence. I often wonder, if I had spoken up, how many could I have saved? I now voice my story in hopes of encouragement and empowerment to the many women and men whose stories reflect similarities with my truth—those who share the physical and emotional fears in the pain of betrayal. I seek my own healing as I release my words. My words tell of betrayal by battle buddies and listening to your intuition. Take heed to the clues.

Healing

I slipped into a state of numbness as a way to cope—my way to survive. You see, this was not my first experience with sexual trauma, so to act as if nothing happened was the only way I knew how to deal with it. As I now look back at my life experiences, I know the numbing was a completely dysfunctional way to deal with my assault.

The first step to healing for me was to start with mirror work; just being able to look at myself without shame or disappointment was huge. That small step later allowed me to work up the courage to confide in a trusted friend, and having just one person to release to saved me. I would also meditate and see a vision of myself being free to counteract my negative thoughts and PTSD around what had happened. Numbing as a survival mechanism can be tricky because it almost allows you to erase your memory. I say *almost* because the traces of the trauma remained, which led me to finally seek help from a psychiatrist.

My healing process is continuous, and even sharing my story in this book has become part of my healing. It really took a lot of soul searching, and I can't even say if I'm 100 percent ready to share this part of my story. What I do know is that it took many years of hard work and self-work to stand strong in my truth. This was not an overnight or impulsive decision. Seeking professional help was imperative to my healing process to the point that I had the courage to publicly share my story outside of the confinement of confidentiality.

I tell my story because I know there are so many more out there like myself: military women who share a similar truth. I want my story to encourage healing and let those who are still silent in the formations know that they are not alone. I know my words will serve others. It is now my mission going forward, as a speaker, to show others that pain has a purpose. My hope is that my story simply lights a path for others to travel toward their own healing.

The most important point I leave with readers is that while I remained silent, I never blamed myself for the reckless actions of others—never! And neither should you! I'm thankful through prayers, faith, and professional counseling that I have come out of camouflage to show my vulnerable scars. They are not easy to reveal, but nevertheless, I stand up! Speak up! Camouflaged no more as the silent survivor, not only in my truth but in your honor!

I pray your restraints be broken to beautiful courage and self-liberation to heal!

7

You Are Valuable

Michelle Dowleyne

Comradery

As I walk down the street, I am always looking behind and around me. I don't like being in dark places by myself. The tree in front of my house has to be cut, so I can see who or what is out there. *What is wrong with me?* Is this normal, or am I just being spooked? Well, that is what I thought until I received my counseling for military sexual trauma. For years, I was haunted by something that was taken from me. It didn't just affect me then; it continues to haunt me every day.

Hanging out in Advanced Individual Training (AIT) was fun and full of laughs. This was the best time to get away and relax, especially after being in Basic Training. This is when we start to build those lasting friendships and really begin to understand what comradery is. For many military, AIT is the first time in eight weeks that we are able to socialize with the opposite sex again. I was always a friendly person and learned to accept people at their face value.

I grew close to several of the male Soldiers in training. We all hung out and had fun together. I looked up to them as my fellow comrades, trusted agents, protectors, and friends. In this environment, we were trained to always have each other's backs and that we were one. Many of us who went through the same training bonded as a group. After spending nearly three months in AIT with this group, I thought I could trust them with my life, and I felt that they had my back.

Friendships Tested

Time moved on, and we all went to Fort Bragg together. I was excited that I didn't have to go to another duty station alone because I had built a great bond with these men and women. A friend in the group moved out of the barracks. It was a big deal to live off post because you had freedom, and no inspections or rules to follow. One Sunday, he invited a few of us over to watch a football game at his house. I was really excited about going because his roommate had expressed interest in me. I thought that we could spend some time together and get to know each other better. We all had fun watching the game together. The roommate asked me if I wanted to stay and said he would get me a ride back to the barracks. I said yes because I thought we were going to hang out some more and talk.

This is the part where the story takes a turn. Keep in mind that I had never been aware of anyone I knew being raped, so in my mind, I did not think that this was a bad decision. I didn't have any reference or reason to be cautious. I knew that my friend from AIT was still there, and this was his roommate, so I wasn't afraid or uncomfortable. Here again, *I trusted these people.* In hindsight, this may have been my biggest mistake.

After everyone left, the roommate invited me into his room to relax and watch TV. I thought to myself, *oh, I am really special, and he likes me.* All evening, he was a perfect gentleman and treated me like a lady, as he had previously. I thought, maybe this could be my first relationship in the army. As we watched TV, he began to fondle me, and I told him to stop because I felt uncomfortable. He became very aggressive, cursing me out, and again, I told him to stop. I wasn't ready. A monster exploded into existence as he pulled me to him and continued to force himself on me. After minutes of me saying no and trying to break free, he told me to get up and get out of his house. I went to my friend's room, knocked on the door, and told him what just happened.

He said he didn't believe it; maybe his roommate was just playing. I went on the porch and cried. My friend finally came outside and gave me a ride back to the barracks.

The toughest thing about being raped is that it lingers in the mind of the victim. The saddest thing is that it can divide friends. As we drove back to post, my friend said he didn't want to get in the middle of it because that was his roommate, and I was his friend. He would talk to him when he got back home. *He encouraged me to let it go and forget about it.* Whoa. I was completely shocked and hurt by his words. I was just raped, but my friend only cared about losing a roommate.

A Lonely Fight

During this time, there was no policy in place where you could report a sexual assault in privacy, and not telling was never an option for me. I returned to the barracks and told a few friends what happened to me after everyone left the house. One of my friends reminded me that one of our other friends worked in the legal office. The next morning, I went to her and told her what had happened. She told me to come to her office and report it, so I did exactly that!

A JAG lawyer interviewed me, asking questions about what happened and who was there. I was told that the assailant would be interviewed and that the JAG office would call the assailant in for questioning and work the case. I only got word that he was being investigated, and there was supposed to be a hearing, but I was never called to appear before any court-martial or do anything after that initial report. It felt as if nothing I said was being taken seriously. Of course, when I went to check on the status of the report, I was told no information could be released to me because now it was his personal case. I'm not sure why I was told this, but as a Private, I took that as an answer, and to this day, I am not sure what punishment he received, if any.

I felt all alone, like maybe I shouldn't have even said anything. Not knowing if anything happened to this guy bothered me, so I reached out to my friend (his roommate) to see if he could tell me anything, but to my surprise, he wouldn't talk to me. He no longer wanted to be associated with me. Sadly, he wasn't the only one from our original group. Funny how the victim becomes the enemy and ends up being the one blamed (this is not funny at all and happens often). It's so disappointing that someone can violate you and take from you, but people choose to support them and turn their back on you. It hurt thinking how this incident divided me and my friends.

Rape is not a disease, but once you speak out, you get treated as if you are the walking dead. Many of my friends didn't believe what happened to me, or they believed that we had consensual sex. I found that strange because a lot of them didn't really know him. We were friends, and we had attended training together, but they chose to side with the roommate. Fellow Soldiers stopped speaking to me as well and disassociated themselves from me. They even told me to stop complaining. As a result of this experience, I now choose to always believe anyone who says their intent was not to have sex, even though they went on a date, went into someone's bedroom, or even laid down with them. It doesn't matter—we have a right to say NO and not be judged because we are in a certain situation.

This left a hole in me that cannot be fixed. The military gives classes on sexual assault prevention, but while sitting in the classes, I would hear whispers from people in the training, laughing and blaming the victim. Throughout my career, it hurt me to hear female friends say, "She asked for it," or "She shouldn't have gone by herself." I would just sit there in silence and cry on the inside because of their ignorant comments. To hear this from friends or fellow female Soldiers really made me take notice of people's lack of education.

My Silent Fight

Throughout my years of service as an NCO, I took on an additional duty as an equal opportunity representative and a unit victim advocate to make sure that the victims had someone to help walk them through the process if they needed to file a claim, and also to make sure the sexual assault training was given in a serious manner. While training, I would be so uncomfortable because of the comments, and I'd have to hold back tears. I wanted to curse people out for negative comments that I heard again and again, but I just suffered in silence. My way of dealing with it was not dealing with it. I just kept it to myself.

I had difficulties in relationships with intimacy. Sex was very emotional for me, and sometimes I would cry because I was still damaged. You see, no matter who believed me among my friends, I had to live with not knowing if I was loved for me or if the guy just wanted me for sex. Rape doesn't just happen that one fateful night; it happens over and over again. Rape is not something you can just get over. How does a fellow Soldier even find it in his mind to take from someone they said they would protect? Did he not have a mother, grandmother, or sister that he loved? What if someone raped them?

Date rape is a real assault, however, many victims are not believed. People feel just because you know the person, you are lying. My message to anyone who may find themselves in this situation is that no matter who you know or where you go, no one has the right to violate you if you say no at any time. Just like you have the right to change your mind about the clothes you are going to wear today, change your mind about the meal you just ordered, or change your mind about purchasing that car, you have the right to change your mind about having sex.

The army eventually came out with this new thing called a unit victim advocate, and for obvious reasons, I jumped at the chance to get the training to become one. I knew what it felt like to feel pain and rejection; to live with the whispers and the system failing you. I felt like this was my way of making sure no one else ever felt like that. Being a victim advocate was my way of silently saying, "I *am* you, and I *believe* you."

I am glad this program is being pushed now and continually improved upon, but it still has a long way to go. I don't know how to completely fix this, but I continue to stress the importance of educating our service men and service women on this subject to protect them. I never shared this with my family because this was the beginning of my military career, and I didn't want them to think badly of the army as a whole because of some system failures.

Once I retired, I called the legal office several times to see if I could get a copy of my records from that case. They referred me to the post sexual assault coordinator, who never called me back. I called several times, and four years later, I still don't have the information. I am not sure if I wanted it for Veterans Affairs or for myself for closure, yet I don't know if closure will truly ever come. I also reached out to three old battle buddies for statements because I knew they were aware of the situation. I received written statements from two friends, but it was hurtful that one, still to this day, said she was sorry and that she didn't know I had been sexually assaulted. This is ironic because she was the one who referred me to our friend who worked for JAG.

Today, I work hard to help women Veterans transform their lives to move forward from past hurts, fears, and wrongs. Women Veterans are unique, and they endure a lot of challenges in silence during their military careers. Today, I am free, and silenced no more.

Your Voice

Merci L. McKinley

Your voice was not made
To be taken away in fear
It's not meant to fade
In the background of your tears

Your voice is not contained
Inside the box your emotions built
It's not meant to be chained
Inside of unjust guilt

It is meant to be spoken
Heard and shouted beyond your pain
It is never beyond repair or broken
Harness it and let it take reign

DEPRESSION, POST-TRAUMATIC STRESS DISORDER, SELF-WORTH

The prettiest smiles hide the deepest secrets. The prettiest eyes have cried the most tears, and the kindest hearts have felt the most pain.

—Unknown

PTSD replaces the "me" who was still growing, learning, and becoming a unique person before the trauma(s), leaving only a desperate survivor who may have no clear sense of identity and who may even hate or loathe herself or himself (www.militarywithptsd.org).

8

Find Your True Self

Lila Holley

My Truth

This could not be happening to me, I thought. I had heard the stories but always thought to myself, *just shake it off. What's wrong with you? It can't be that hard.* Well, I soon found out that depression is not something you can just "shake off."

I had a conversation that I can laugh about now, but at the time, it was not very funny. I was at the Veteran's hospital finishing up the last part of my physical for my disability claim. The doctor was going to check out my shoulder and finish up my paperwork to complete my claim. I walked into his office, and we went through some stretching and range-of-motion drills before I had a seat next to his desk.

We began small talk, and I soon found out that he had never served in the military but focused his studies on post-traumatic stress disorder (PTSD) with regard to trauma experienced later in life. For example, he studied those who had survived car accidents and other traumatic experiences as adults. His studies also covered adults who had lost parents and the impact of that traumatic loss on these adults. I found this interesting and asked, "How did you end up at the VA serving Veterans?" He said he wanted the opportunity to research PTSD even further and thought this would be a great environment to do so.

He asked me what I did in the military, did I deploy, and did I miss it now that I was retired? I answered, "I was a Military Intelligence Warrant Officer. Yes, one long deployment and two short deployments." I paused before I went on to answer his last question, "Yes, I guess I do miss it." As we talked some more, I shared with him that it really surprised me how much I missed the military. Not the military per say, I clarified, but the people I had met and the organized system that I had mastered and succeeded in. I felt pretty comfortable talking with him when I said these words out loud: "I actually find myself crying often for no apparent reason."

Did I really just say that?

Yes, I sure did. This was the first person, besides my husband, to whom I had admitted that I was having trouble adjusting to life outside the uniform.

He didn't even look up from his paperwork when he said to me, "You know, crying for no apparent reason is not normal."

I wanted to say "No shit, Sherlock!" but I opted for "I *know* that," as I nervously chuckled and fought back tears.

He was pulling together articles for me to read to help me better understand PTSD and depression. We continued to talk a little more, and I left his office knowing I had to do something. I needed help to figure out why I was feeling like this.

Fast forward, and I find myself in a mental health counselor's office. I was a little nervous. This was the very first time I had spoken to a mental health counselor. I probably could have benefitted from seeing one sooner. Who am I kidding? There is no "probably" about it. I know I should have seen a counselor well before then. I would go as far as to say maybe even during my twenty-two-year army career. But that was taboo—something officers just didn't do. I was not willing to do anything that would jeopardize my security clearance, so I paid my bills, and I stayed away from mental health.

Anyway, I found myself in her office, a little nervous but willing to try this counseling thing out. I went in knowing that I did not want to be medicated, as I did not feel my situation warranted that type of treatment. So we began to talk, and she asked me questions about my career: did I deploy, what was I doing now, etc.? You know, easy questions. Questions I could answer in my sleep.

Then it happened. She asked me that one question that stopped me in my tracks: "Who is Lila?"

"Huh? I just told you who I am. I'm the chief, leader, Soldier."

"No ma'am, that's who Lila was. Who is Lila now? Now that Lila has taken off the uniform and picked up the title Veteran, retired Veteran?"

"Hmmm, good question," I said, to buy me a little more time.

I soon found myself crying and blowing my nose talking about fifteen-year-old, pregnant Lila who struggled with self-esteem issues. What the hell just happened here, Lady! Apparently, I had some unresolved issues in my life that had brought me to this point, sitting in the office of a mental health counselor.

I was diagnosed with depression. Although mild (in my mind), it was a diagnosis. I could say I was a step ahead, as I had already started implementing some tools to help me move past this period of sadness, but my truth: I was dealing with depression.

I never thought this would be me. I went through periods of sadness throughout my life, but who hasn't? I had gotten so good at suppressing my emotions (I mastered stepping on my emotions with my combat boots) and burying them to be dealt with at a later time. It was only now in my transition from the military that I came to terms with the fact that I had not fully dealt with many of my emotionally driven life events. The truth was, I had life situations that I had never effectively processed, nor did I have a healthy manner of processing my emotions, hence the outbursts of crying for no apparent reason.

Going to this counselor's office really helped me put a name to what I was experiencing and feeling. But what I was really seeking were the tools to help me manage my emotions and move forward in my transition process.

Calm Down

So how did I get here? Well, it was a gradual progression. When I look back at how everything transpired, how I ended up in that counselor's office, it was such a gradual process. The changes in my behavior were so minimal that when others started to notice, it seemed like I had changed overnight. I was good at hiding the symptoms. It was 2012, and I was ecstatic about retirement. I was heading back to New York, close to my family. We were excited about the opportunity for our daughter to spend time with both sets of grandparents and a great-grandmother; not many military kids get this type of opportunity. To be honest, I was a little apprehensive. I had been away from home for over twenty-two years while in the military.

I brushed those feelings to the side and looked to the future with hope and excitement because I would be helping out with a family restaurant, which had always been a dream of mine. We arrived in New York, and the adventure began.

The first thing I noticed was that everyone moved so slow around here. There was no sense of urgency about anything. I gave my grandmother an alibi—she was ninety-three, so she had earned the right to move slowly. But everyone else had no excuse, so I had to learn to readjust my day-to-day pace. I was used to the adrenalin rush of a busy army day, and life outside the military was different. I worked hard to create a normal pattern for myself, starting with my morning workout on the treadmill while watching my morning news show. This helped, but only a little.

It didn't get any better at the restaurant. Usually, you have to have a sense of urgency when serving people, and I came in with that sense of urgency. I was ready, moving fast and efficiently, taking orders, and anticipating what our customers would need if they were dining in or taking their food to go.

One weekend, we were double booked for two parties, a leadership breakfast for a group of local pastors and a baby shower in the afternoon. This was a good day. I loved when we were busy. I knocked the breakfast out like a champ. All attendees were pleased, bellies were full, and the meeting agenda completed.

Time to transition.

I began calling out time hacks so the team on the floor could stay on task to complete everything that needed to be done before the beaming mother-to-be walked in. I went back to the kitchen, reviewed the preapproved menu one more time, and went over time hacks for certain food items to be ready to move to the buffet line. I was in the zone, like a senior NCO preparing her team for a mission. Get 'er done!

Then I heard the words, calm down.

Huh? I didn't understand. Calm down? We have a timeline to meet. Calming down will be done when we have completed the task for today: execute two successful parties. We are halfway there, and now is not the time to calm down. I blew it off and went back on to the floor: "Time check—11:30! Let's go team! Looking good!"

Time is moving along, and things are shaping up nicely. The tables are arranged, decorations are in place, and the buffet line is set and ready for displaying food. I make my way back to the kitchen to check on the progress being made. Well, things were moving along—not as fast as I would have liked, but moving along nonetheless. "Things are looking good in here. I'll prepare the dessert trays," I say out loud but really to myself. I get that done, and the family of the expecting mother starts pouring into the restaurant. I go to greet them, put up the last of the decorations, and go over the games to be played. This was going to be a great party.

A few food items are still missing from the buffet line. *Hmmm,* I think to myself, heading back into the kitchen. I must have had a look of panic on my face because the first thing I hear is, "Calm down." Again, not really understanding, so I dismiss the comment and ask about the status of the fried chicken wings. "Seven more minutes. We'll get them out there. Calm down, this is not the army."

At which I reply, "This is me, calm, right here, at this level of intensity. We have a party to execute to a level of standard for this family who has trusted us with the celebration of this special occasion."

"Well, calm down, we'll get it done," was the response.

This became the most common phrase in the restaurant: "Calm down, Lila." I felt like I might snap if one more person told me to "calm down." There was definitely going to be a situation if I heard one more "calm down." I began to examine why this was being said to me so often. Was something wrong with me? No. Surely there was nothing wrong with me.

Something Had to Change

As a result of this experience, I began to change. I actually did try to calm down, lay back, be cool, or whatever other phrase you can think of to describe this state of being. The problem was that my calm didn't look like those around me. My calm came with high intensity.

I began to bite my tongue, talk a little less, and hold things inside in order to keep the peace. This is when the crying began. It took place at night when I would go to bed early by myself. I would grab my pillow and soak it with my tears—tears that held the words I wanted to scream in anger to those around me. I had questions and no one to ask them to. Why doesn't anyone understand me? Why do I miss the military so much? Why does everyone want me to be someone I am not? I held these questions inside day in and day out, only to release them into my pillow.

That is until I couldn't do it anymore. I soon began to display signs of someone who struggled with anger issues. I was short with my loved ones, snappy in my tone and conversation with them. This was not me or my normal demeanor. I needed an outlet, and anger seemed to be as good as any. I figured it would help me feel a little better about my unanswered questions.

Anger is never a good outlet.

It didn't make me feel good. It actually made matters worse. I didn't even recognize this woman I had turned into. I knew something had to change. Anger was actually a symptom for a deeper problem I was dealing with. I decided to write my family members letters, trying to explain what was going on inside of me. Funny thing is, I didn't even fully understand what was going on with me until I sought out counseling. With my family, I shared the feelings I was struggling with. The feelings I had about missing the military. The feelings I had about realizing that my family didn't know the incredible woman I had grown into as a result of my military career. I wanted them to get to know her because she's *me*. I felt like they wanted me to be someone I was not. I felt like they didn't even give me a chance. I felt sad and rejected. Once I shared this revelation with my family, the lines of communication opened up and began to improve.

I began to walk in my truth. I felt my power come back as I began to make decisions that were in my best interest. My mental health became a priority, and this was when I decided to seek counseling. My decision to take action came because I felt if I didn't do something, I risked destroying relationships that I valued tremendously. I wasn't willing to risk that. I wasn't going to let anger destroy my family. It has been quite a journey, and I have learned so much about myself. I still have highly emotional days; on these days, my tear ducts overflow. It's on these days I have to make a choice: do I win or do I let depression win? I am glad to say my wins significantly outnumber depression's wins.

9

Encourage Yourself

Teresa Robinson

My Military Journey

When I joined the military twenty-three years ago, I never imagined the journey that I would experience. I was a young nineteen-year-old who had never traveled outside of the state of Louisiana. I was about to complete two years of college at Southern University-Shreveport and wanted to make a change, especially since my two-year scholarship was about to end. After talking to a recruiter, taking the Armed Services Vocational Aptitude Battery (ASVAB), and choosing to pursue a medical career, I told my family of my plans. They were not happy at first, but they became receptive as the time neared for me to depart for Basic Training. I was scared and excited at the same time about the journey I was about to experience.

After attending Basic Training and Advanced Individual Training (AIT), I became a medical laboratory specialist and received my first duty assignment at Madigan Army Medical Center in Fort Lewis, Washington. I was very excited about my new experiences. I joined the laboratory team and learned so much as a Soldier and technician working in the various departments of pathology. One thing that really surprised me was seeing autopsies being performed on human beings. I didn't expect that. The first time I saw an autopsy, I was in total shock. I had to pump myself up and say to myself, it's part of your job. I couldn't believe the process of the deceased human body. One day you're here, and the next day, you transition to the other side.

The Trauma of Death and Loss

Even though I accepted that death and loss would be a regular part of my job while in the military, I never truly got used to the fact. I had dealt with the death of a high school classmate, who my siblings and I grew up with in the same neighborhood. This was the first real experience with death where I truly understood the finality of it. He was a popular high school basketball player, and I was one of the female scorekeepers who traveled with the team. We were seniors in high school and participated in many activities together.

On Easter Sunday in 1990, he was shot while playing basketball in the park. He was an innocent bystander.

I rushed to the hospital after hearing that he had been shot. My siblings, classmates, and I all went to the chapel to pray that he would survive this horrific crime. Unfortunately, he did not.

After learning that he had passed, we could not sleep for days. It felt like the city went into a standstill for weeks after his death. I tried to process the death of my friend internally, but now I realize that I just settled with suppressing my emotions about his death in order to keep going. This was a skill I soon came to master.

The next traumatic experience with death occurred while serving overseas, when I lost our infant son due to stillborn birth. Within weeks, while still on convalescent leave, I lost my grandfather. The loss of my son made me feel so lost and hurt, while the loss of my grandfather broke a special bond with someone I loved dearly. I didn't understand why this was happening to me. I was very close to my grandfather, having lived with him part of my high school years. He was very influential in my life. I still miss them both every day.

After the losses, someone told me that I had to "get over it and move on." I was very upset by these words. I felt this advice was insensitive considering I had experienced such significant losses around the same time. It takes time to get over losing a child, and to be honest, I don't think you ever fully get over it. As a parent, you learn how to manage your emotions, and you hope to move forward. I carried my son for seven months, and we bonded. He did not survive, and someone has the nerve to tell me to get over it? I could not believe it. Those words hurt me deeply.

Sometimes it feels as if it happened yesterday. The chaplain came and said a prayer with us. The nursing staff allowed me to spend the last moments with him. As I prepared to leave the hospital, I was provided a purple box filled with special memories: photos, ID bracelet, baptism certificate, and a special empathy card signed by the NICU staff. I was very thankful to the nursing staff, chaplain, and chain of command, who all helped me make it through the process a little easier. The compassion they showed toward me was heartfelt, and I appreciated their efforts. As we prepared to bury our child, I heard so many sayings from people:

It wasn't meant to be.

God knows best.

Everything happens for a reason.

Although I knew the people saying these things to me didn't mean any harm, their words were not comforting. I felt terrible after hearing those types of comments.

I've learned from this experience that you have to show empathy, and if you don't know what to say, give a hug or a card.

The Trauma of Losing My Mother

My next experience with loss was devastating; it shook me to the core of my being. The loss of my mother was very traumatic. Although I knew she was suffering from a disease that would eventually take her life, I was not emotionally prepared for her death. She was very strong and brave until the end. She called early on June 27, 2012, stating she was being admitted to the hospital. I told her I would be there in two to three hours, factoring in that I had to notify my command and travel. When I arrived, she seemed okay, but she was in pain.

On the second day of her hospital stay, she was in good spirits, talking and eating, but she started showing signs of anxiety. My sibling and I tried to comfort her as much as we could. As the night approached, we prepared for bed. I climbed in her hospital bed with her, and we said our prayers. I told her I loved her, and she said she loved me. I told her I would never leave her. She proceeded to say, "Make sure you take my yellow bag with you."

I asked her, "What did you say?" And she repeated the statement.

The yellow bag symbolized my mom letting me know she was leaving us and that she wanted me to take her personal belongings. I had never been so scared before in my life. I called my twin sister to tell her what was going on. She immediately came up to the hospital. She said, "Mom is not going to be here with us much longer."

We stayed up praying and watching her, hoping that things would get better. But she was slowly going into a deep sleep, battling with the other side. We could hear her calling out her deceased mother and father's names. I could not understand or grasp entirely what was happening so quickly. She had taken a turn for the worse, and the doctor confirmed my worst nightmare. *There was nothing more they could do.*

Family members visited throughout the day and night, providing support and comfort, and my Mom passed away the next night. My heart was forever broken. I could not stop crying. I kept asking God, "Why did You take my mom so young?" I was blessed with a son after the previous pregnancy loss, and I wanted my mom to see her youngest grandchild grow up. I had so much I wanted to do with her as I was nearing the time to retire from the military.

As I faced the daunting task of planning her funeral, I was heartbroken. All I could do was think about the process I knew her body would have to go through once she was taken to the funeral home. While I know this is the standard procedure for processing bodies, I wanted my mother to be honored in a special way because she loved everyone and opened her heart and home to anyone in need. I now realize I was experiencing the shock and denial phase of grief. I had not yet fully come to terms with the fact that my mother had passed away.

My Reality: Life then Death

Death and loss remained a consistent part of my life and career for years. I felt like it was always occurring around me. I lost a friend who was found deceased in his barrack's room. And then another friend who committed suicide because he couldn't deal with what he felt were unbearable life situations. When death occurs, my thoughts immediately go to the excruciating pain that devastated family members are left to deal with in the aftermath.

I can say that my job as a medical laboratory technician was both rewarding and demanding. Demanding in that there were so many instances of death resulting from various causes. One instance that sticks out the most is when I had to prepare the remains of an infant who was stillborn. The parents wanted to spend some time in their private room. The first autopsy I experienced was the spouse of a Soldier who had passed away from unknown reasons. She had requested to donate one of her organs—her eyeballs—which were replaced with marbles after the procedure.

Over time, my emotions grew numb after seeing so many autopsies, and I began to focus more on the technicality of the procedure. The pathologists start the autopsy by observing the overall appearance of the body. The first cut is from shoulder to shoulder and then straight down the body like a letter T. Then each organ (heart, lungs, stomach, small and large intestines, etc.) is removed, evaluated, and weighed. They are placed in a container for testing. Then the pathologist proceeds to the head, cutting a line from ear to ear, pulling the skin back, revealing the skull. The skull is then cut, and the brain is removed. Once all organs are removed, each area is sewn back together to look whole. Upon completion of the autopsy, the remains are returned to the body bag and stored until respectfully prepared and transferred to Mortuary Affairs or the designated funeral home.

Focusing on the mechanics became easier for me than it was to process the reasons bodies ended up in the morgue to begin with. After seeing so many losses of service members who died from suicide, unknown causes, motor vehicle accidents, gunshot wounds, alcohol, and drug overdoses, I had grown numb. *My emotions left me incapable of action.*

Learning to Cope with Loss

Once my emotions went numb, it was very hard to cope with the loss of friends and loved ones. Loss became my turning point. I felt that my life was forever changed with each experience of loss, both from my personal and professional life. How would I continue on and enjoy life? I couldn't eat, sleep, drink, think, or function as I used to. I prayed and hoped it was just a dream that I would wake up from. The fear and the thoughts of death overtook my mind. I couldn't control the anxiety. I couldn't close my eyes to sleep because of the visions I would see. The sounds of voices calling my name awakened me from sleep. The biggest issue I struggled with was the loss of memory, which makes me fear dementia will eventually set in.

I fell into a deep depression. I felt like I was in a constant state of grief and mourning. There are seven stages of grief:

1. Shock

2. Pain

3. Anger

4. Depression

5. Upward turn

6. Reconstruction

7. Acceptance

I believe I am currently stuck in the depression phase. I share my story not only to help myself move forward in the healing process but to encourage someone else who may be struggling with loss. I still have so many questions. Why did this have to happen to me? What did I do wrong? Am I being punished? Each day, I wish I could have one more day to talk, hug, smell, and kiss each one of my loved ones who died. Some days, it is hard to function, but I have to push through and work to manage my emotions. I know I will get through it as long as I surround myself with positivity and good support—and so will YOU. Do not isolate yourself. I know firsthand that isolation does not work, and it can really push you deeper into depression.

One day, I realized that we all have a true gift from God: *memories*. At first, I didn't know why God created memories, but I soon realized that those memories could help with the healing process. So as I continue to take it one day at a time, I cope with my medical condition by making sure I take my medication as required and schedule my appointments to talk to my counselor. I strive to live life to the fullest, and I recommend that you do the same. Make sure you show your loved ones that you care about them while they are alive. Love them unconditionally, take a lot of pictures, and create wonderful memories. We all will experience death and handle it our way. When that time comes, just take it one day at a time.

10

Forgive Yourself

Ivy Edwards

That Glow

I joined the military in 1988 and was activated for Desert Storm in 1990. At that time, I had only known two people in my family that had actually served in a war, and they were males: my father and grandfather. Listening to their stories as a little girl, I felt so far-removed. I couldn't relate. I could only listen. Now, all of a sudden, we would be connected on a different level, and I would have similar experiences. Though I never asked for advice, I received advice from various family members and friends. Most notably, my father and his good friend, who told me something that really stuck with me: *"It's a thin line between having your mind and losing it."*

At the time I went to Desert Storm, my grandfather was in the hospital and was terrified at the thought of the country being at war. I couldn't imagine what it would do to him to find out his young granddaughter would be going. I never got the chance to tell him. He passed shortly after the war started.

Even though I didn't have many family members or personal acquaintances who could advise me about war, I had a group of people that, just like me, were going through something they had never experienced. I joined the 183rd PSC. This was my unit, and we were family. Just like with any family, some members form a closer bond than others. We were called Tent #1! The females in this tent formed an unbreakable, sisterly bond.

On Sunday, March 3, 1991, one of my sisters, Pamela Gay, went to church. Afterward, she told us all about how she found Jesus and that she was getting baptized the following Sunday. She was so excited! She wrote a letter home to her parents telling them how she found Jesus and how happy she was. She asked me to proofread the letter. I told her that it sounded great, but I advised her to take the part out about how she would be home for her birthday because we didn't know when we were going home. Her birthday was April 26. The next Sunday, March 10, was the day of her baptism. All of her closest friends were seated on the front row. She had this glow about her. I'd never seen someone actually glow before. I felt like that glow was Jesus, all up and through her!

After the ceremony, people who had come to support her formed a long line to hug her. I didn't get in the line, and afterward, she asked me why. I said, "I can hug you anytime. We sleep in the same tent." We left the ceremony and took a picture with her in front of the mess hall (church) where she was just baptized.

Our Commander asked Pam if she wanted to go take some supplies to the rest of our unit, closer to Kuwait. She said, "I'll go if Ivy goes." I agreed, thinking that if she didn't want to go at all, she would have just said it. So we all loaded up onto this two-and-a-half-ton truck headed toward Kuwait, less than an hour after she was baptized. We just talked for what seemed like hours. Everyone else must have been asleep. We talked about some of everything. We talked of having a big party when we returned home. She even asked me why I wore that ragged scarf. I told her that it belonged to my mother, who had passed a few years earlier, so it had sentimental value to me.

That Night

We returned to the truck. She and I had been trading spaces back and forth between the floor and the bench. This was her time to get on the bench, and I was on the floor beside her. I told her that I was afraid to fall asleep because I felt like the large grill would fall on me. It was a large charcoal grill. We were taking it to our troops, and it was in the bed of the truck that we were in.

She said, "It's going to fall as long as you're thinking about it." Minutes later, I must have dozed off. I heard a loud noise, and then I felt something hit my head.

That night is very vague to me, and I only remember bits and pieces. I was standing over Pam as she held the bottom of my leg. She kept telling me that she was dying. I told her she wasn't dying, and we still had to have the welcome home party we had just discussed. I was shaking tremendously. Another Soldier, who suffered a serious injury to her leg, said, "Whoever is on the truck shaking, can they please keep still?" I was no more than 125 pounds, and I had a two-and-a-half-ton truck shaking!

We treated Pam for shock. We splinted the other Soldier's (Sandra) leg with my mother's scarf. All of the Soldiers stepped up to the plate and did what we were trained to do: *assess the damage and treat your fellow Soldiers.* I got off of the truck, and I could not feel my face, but I could taste blood. I asked Nina what was wrong with my face. She said nothing was wrong with my face and that everything was fine. I imagine I was pretty panicked after I got off of the truck because I said to her, "You can tell me what's wrong with my face. I won't go into shock!" To this day, we laugh that I was already in shock.

An ambulance finally arrived on the scene (a small, Blazer-type truck) and transported Pam and Sandra to the hospital. They tried to get me to go, but I refused. This was a very small truck, and I'm claustrophobic. Besides, I couldn't imagine how my unit would ever find me because I didn't know exactly where they'd be taking us. Nope, no thanks. I'll just continue the ride toward Kuwait. Our vehicle was still drivable, and after they were taken away in the ambulance, we had to continue the mission.

Nina went to the hospital with them. As we returned to the truck, I heard someone say, "Don't let her go to sleep!" I was slapped and pushed for what seemed like hours to keep me from falling asleep. We arrived at our location and informed everyone of the accident. A large tractor trailer was carrying a tank. We were in the right-hand lane, going in the opposite direction. We were driving as far to the right as we could, without driving in the sand because the oncoming vehicles were so close. The tractor was very large and moving at a high rate of speed. The vehicle never even slowed down after it hit us. We think our vehicle was hit by the knobs on the tank. We were informed that Sandra had a broken leg and would be flown to Germany. Everything was quiet—just stone silence.

Now, I, in my bright twenty-one-year-old mind, figured that since he didn't tell us about Pam, who he knew was closest to us, there must have been a real problem. I didn't want to ask the question, how is Pam? I felt like if I didn't hear it, it wasn't true. One of the other Soldiers asked, and I was not prepared for what came next: "Pam—" sniffle...sniffle..."She didn't make it!" Everyone in the tent burst into tears. Grown men crying out loud! We all were. This was truly one of the worst nights of my life.

That Pain

We held a memorial service for her, and again, we were on the front row. It was so surreal. About a week earlier, she was standing in this very spot, glowing and getting baptized, and now we were looking at her boots and helmet. I couldn't fathom what was going on. I said a poem and did not know who was standing beside me holding me up until I saw the tape months later. I couldn't even pick my head up. I felt like the weight of the world was on my shoulders. I felt emotions that I didn't know I had.

I had questions that I wanted answers to: How could she just leave like that? Why did God have to take her like that? Why did I agree to get on that truck? It didn't take me long to come to grips with the first two questions. The pastor's advice to me was, "in the midst of seven people, God chose her. She was ready, and God makes no mistakes." It was then that I believed she made it home for her birthday. But I would go on to struggle with the last question for years.

I spent years blaming myself for her death. I had so many unanswered questions and no one to turn to for the answers. Why did I get on that truck? She said she would go if I went. If I hadn't gone, she'd still be alive. Why didn't I stay in the seat? Had I been in that seat, she'd still be alive. Why did she say that she was dying? How do you know when you're dying? What does it feel like? Why did she leave that part in her letter that she would be home for her birthday after I told her to remove it? Why didn't I hug her after she got baptized? What I wouldn't give now for a hug from her. Why did she say the grill would hit me? Why didn't I want to hear what happened to her? Was I as good of a friend to her as I felt she was to me? So many unanswered questions. I felt so alone, and I became very depressed.

For years, I didn't even talk about the accident and blamed everything that went wrong in my life afterward on the bad decisions I made earlier. Karma. It was like the universe was saying to me, "There you go again, making more bad decisions." My inner self was my most critical self. I didn't love myself, so I didn't think that I was worthy of love. I didn't even think I deserved love. I realize now that at that point in my life, I allowed people to treat me like I *thought* I deserved to be treated. I just felt like a part of me was a very bad person. People with hurtful intensions are like vultures. They know when you're down and out, and they will feed on you.

A few years ago, I woke up on a Monday morning with a dull pain in my stomach. The pain intensified every couple of hours, so I decided to go to the emergency room. They checked me out, gave me some IV fluids, and sent me home. I asked for pain medication, but they did not give me any. Now, anyone who really knows me knows I don't do pain medicine. My husband was shocked that I had even asked. I came home, crying and in pain. I called back to the emergency room, and the nurse said, "Baby, if you're in that much pain, you shouldn't have left." It took me twelve hours to get to the bathroom, take a shower, and return to the hospital. The pain was almost unbearable. I had become delusional at this point. I believed that I was in labor—nevermind the fact that my tubes had been tied for over five years. Again, I was sent home, but this time, they gave me a Tylenol as I departed.

When I got home, I just had this feeling that I wouldn't last much longer. I actually felt like I was dying. Right there, God had just answered a question that I had for years. Why would Pam say she was dying? How did it feel? Immediately, I knew I had to get back to the hospital. Something clicked inside of me at that moment. I realized *I AM important, I AM worthy of love, and my life IS worth fighting for!* No longer would I sit on the sidelines of my life and not be an active participant!

Back at the hospital, I explained my symptoms to a third triage nurse. I believe God placed an angel beside this nurse in the form of another triage nurse who was working on another patient at the time. When he heard my responses to the routine questions, he instantly knew the problem and stepped in. This angel gently touched my back and said, "Mrs. Edwards, we're going to make sure you're all better when you leave here." This was music to my ears! More importantly, it confirmed that I *had* to become an active participant in my life in order to survive! No one can tell your story like you can, so if you don't speak it, no one will know it. I couldn't explain my symptoms in medical terms, but I know that telling my story of my symptoms and how I was feeling saved my life. *In less than fifteen minutes, I was in surgery for a ruptured appendix!* This experience was the beginning of a healing process for me in so many ways.

There comes a time when you have to turn to and completely trust God! I had to stop looking for answers to the questions and trust that God would provide them in His timing. Just let go and let God. Today, I love me! Yes, I'm still a work in progress, but at least I'm open and available for God to work on! For many years, I didn't feel like I was anything! God loves me, and I know He makes no mistakes. *He takes the best to warn the rest.* This profound statement was said at Pam's memorial, but I wasn't ready to receive it then. Now, over twenty years after that service, I receive it, I embrace it, and I live a full life in honor of my dear friend.

Do I miss Pam? Absolutely. I miss her today as much as I did when she first passed away. It's on the tough days that I know where my help cometh from. I know I am here for a reason. He kept me, in the midst of it all. I can look back and see the one footprint in the sand, and I know for sure, those were the times He was carrying me!

11

Love Yourself

Lakisha Coles

God's Love Is Sufficient

Growing up in church, I have always known that God has a purpose for each and every one of us. My mom made us attend morning, afternoon, and evening services, so it is safe to say that I was a faithful churchgoer. I am writing this chapter to encourage each and every one of you to know who you are and whose you are: God's child. I also want you to take from my experience that self-love is the best way to receive all of God's love. I want you to realize that His love is sufficient, and there's no man, woman, boy, or girl that will ever take His place—ever. He will be there for you no matter what. He never judges you, and as long as you continue to seek Him, everything else shall come to pass. Matthew 6:33 states, "But seek first his kingdom and his righteousness, and all these things will be given to you as well."

A little over thirty-six years ago, a star was born. I, Lakisha Renee Carter, was born November 19, in Baltimore, Maryland. That's all I know about my birth. You see, I never really knew who my birth parents were because they weren't the people who raised me. I have heard many stories about my mom and dad, but I'm not sure how true any of them are because I was too young to remember. I never understood why my birth parents gave me up for adoption; well, I have some sense of why. I was told that my birth mom and dad were habitual drug users. I was adopted at the tender age of three, and my name was changed to Lakisha Renee Coles.

My adopted family and I were never the family who always said, "I love you," before going to bed, before heading to school, or even just because. It wasn't important to me back then, but as I grew older, I realized how those little things would affect the rest of my life. I would never lie to you and say I had a rough upbringing, but I will say that I was the kid who had to be in the house before the streetlights came on.

I was never taught about womanhood or how to be a lady. I learned everything from experience. I was blessed enough to graduate from Western Senior High School in 1997 and immediately started a career in the fast food industry. I loved making money, and I worked hard for it, but I wanted to do something different. I was ready to be on my own and make my own decisions. I decided to join the US Army.

Becoming an Adult

I went to the MEP Station (military entrance processing station) to get shipped out to Basic Training in Fort Jackson, South Carolina. I had all types of mixed emotions. I went from being happy that I joined the military to being scared because I didn't know what I had gotten myself into. I had no idea where my life was headed! I just wanted to be on my own when I decided to join the US Army Reserves as an automated logistical specialist in the summer of 1997. So off to Basic Training I went.

The next eight weeks were tough: road marches, very early mornings, Drill Sergeants yelling and screaming in my face. Ahhh, the perfect life. In August 1997, it was time. I graduated from Basic Training, and I was officially a Soldier in the US Army. My job was to protect and serve the president and the people of the United States. Wow, what a task! Less than 8 percent of the US population have signed their names on the dotted line to sacrifice their lives for the freedom of others, and *I was one of them.* What an honor!

After finishing Basic Training, I headed to Advanced Individual Training (AIT) in Fort Lee, Virginia, which was very close to my home. During AIT, we were taught our individual jobs. I spent a few months in AIT and headed back home to Baltimore. I decided to work a regular nine to five. You'll never guess where I went back to work: McDonald's. I loved it. It was fast and easy, no resumes, and more importantly, no interviews. Being in the Army Reserve meant that I would spend time with my unit once a month and two weeks out of the summer for training. My reserve unit was in Glen Burnie, Maryland. The Army Reserves was great, but I wanted more and decided to become an active-duty Soldier. I reenlisted in the US Army active service and was stationed in Germany for my first assignment. I was so excited because I was free! I was officially on my own, and as a young adult, that's the most exciting feeling in the world! I didn't realize it at the time, but there was only one thing missing.

Being in an adopted family, I always felt that I didn't completely belong, in a way. There were times when my brother would tell me to "get off his mother," as if to say she wasn't my mom as well. He was her biological son and me being adopted weighed heavy on my soul when he said that. He was a kid though—what did kids know back then? But what he didn't know was that it hurt. He didn't have to give me a reminder of what I wasn't. This feeling was brought on by many things, but the main thing that contributed to what I felt was the *lack of love.*

First Shot of Love

I headed off to Germany at the tender age of nineteen, and I was super excited about starting this new chapter in my life. While stationed in Germany from 1999 to 2001, I had an awesome time meeting new people, learning to become a leader, and enjoying life overall. I also missed my family. After my tour in Germany, I was blessed to be assigned to my first stateside duty station at Fort Bragg in Fayetteville, North Carolina. That's where I met him.

We were preparing to deploy to support Operation Iraqi Freedom, and at that time, he was my only support system. I had my family back in Baltimore, but he was there in the physical form. When he and I first started dating, I felt like it was love at first sight. We were in Afghanistan, and we were each other's backbones. I was down for him, and he was down for me. We spent a lot of time together getting to know one another, and as time went on, I grew to find my first true love—or so I thought. I spent the next couple of years growing, learning, and spending a lot of time with him. You may question if our relationship was perfect. Of course not, but I loved exactly where we were.

Doomed

By the time we reached our two-year anniversary, the relationship took a turn for the worse. He was getting ready to get out of the military, and I was ready to be shipped off to Korea for a one-year assignment. I assured him that I had his back no matter what. I was his ride-or-die chick, and we were unstoppable together. All of a sudden, he started to act a little differently. He started seeing other women behind my back, and I didn't understand why. *What was wrong with me?* I always blamed myself for his mistakes. During these tough times in our relationship, I would think about how my birth parents had given me up for adoption. I felt the need to fight for my relationship. I wasn't a quitter! I could never give up on the very thing that I had been longing for for years: LOVE.

But that wasn't love. In my mind, I thought it was because I had never experienced it growing up. It simply had to be! My thoughts on love were likely distorted because of the lack of love in my family. I accepted what he gave me in this relationship to define what love was. See, as women, we tend to try and figure out what we've done wrong to make our relationships go south. *Why was I blaming myself? After all, I didn't cheat on him!*

The last six months of my tour in Korea, things started to get even worse. He had stopped calling, and we had all but lost contact. My calls and emails went unanswered. When I returned back to the United States, our relationship was a little different than before. I often asked him if everything was okay, but he always answered with an "I'm fine."

He seemed to grow distant, but I continued to do the right thing as a girlfriend and be there for him no matter what. He started a new job, and at times, he would not come home. I would often wait up for him at night, only to be disappointed. I was told by a couple of friends that they saw him in different places that he never told me about. We started arguing a lot, and that's when I realized that the man I fell in love with was definitely a different man from the one who stood in front of me.

I received a lot of verbal abuse from him. Now, I know some of you may say, "at least he didn't physically harm you," but verbal abuse is just as bad as physical abuse. He often told me that no one would ever want me besides him. The crazy thing was, I believed him! *I believed that no one would love me.* I believed that he was the best man I could have ever met. The real problem was, I didn't believe in me. He would belittle me, make fun of me, and be very disrespectful toward me. I often blamed myself for why he treated me the way he did. I would often make up excuses to trick my mind into thinking that what he was doing was okay. But it was not okay. *Abuse is abuse, and if you allow it to happen, it will.*

Depression Sets In

There were times when he would call me out of my name, or he would say very cruel things to me about my weight. It's funny how some women struggle with losing weight, and here I am, insecure because I couldn't gain any. I would try so hard to gain weight by binge eating and taking weight gainers just to get him to love me again.

I started to lose myself. I started to dislike myself. I actually started to hate myself.

I didn't understand why he had fallen out of love with me. I often blamed myself, time and time again, for his unacceptable behavior. One thing I never realized was, during those years of pain, cheating, verbal abuse, and lies, I was unhappy with my relationship. I was unhappy with everything around me. I was unhappy with myself. I was unhappy with the way I looked, and I was unhappy with the way I felt, all because someone else was unhappy with me.

Time for a Change

During this time, I was talking to my best friend, and she made me look in a mirror. She said, "Look at yourself. You are awesome. You are beautiful. You don't need a man to justify you. *You justify you.*" Ever since that day, it stuck. I am beautiful! I am awesome!

I went to church and asked God why these things were happening to me. I asked Him why I had those feelings about myself. I prayed to God daily to take those negative thoughts out of my head. I prayed and prayed, asking God to teach me how to love myself. I actually waited until I heard an answer from him. God told me that His love is more than enough. He said, "Yes, my child, my love is enough."

See, the one thing I realized was, I can't love anybody else if I can't love myself. Once I received that message and believed it for myself, I began to love myself again. After that self-evaluation, I knew that God was the key to my happiness. Yes, GOD! As women, sometimes we rely on men or even others to validate us, when the complete opposite is true. God is our Provider, Protector, Confidant, Father, and Healer. He's there when we need someone to talk to, and guess what? He doesn't judge! I'm not sure what your beliefs are, but just know that God loves you and so do I!

A Journey

Merci L. McKinley

A journey is made of many things
The constant climb to rise
A story that yearns to sing
That internal flame that never dies

It is not without doubts
In self or battles no one sees
Tugging at how to figure a way out
Low moments that bring you to your knees

A journey is made when you are clear
To travel lessons no matter how long or its length
Taking leaps and bounds beyond fears
With an amazing amount of strength

A journey is constant and an evolution
That brings you from your knees to your feet
It is to find beauty in the solution of your motivation
It is never complete until you refuse to submit to defeat

THE ROAD TO HEALING

It has been said, "time heals all wounds." I do not agree. The wounds remain. In time, the mind, protecting its sanity, covers them with scar tissue and the pain lessens. But it is never gone.

—Rose Fitzgerald Kennedy

This book is intended to help in the healing process of those who read it and find similarities within their own stories. The women who released their stories on these pages are just like you: sisters in arms; leaders; patriots; NCOs; officers; military women whose stories are incredible, just like yours. Military women who, just like you, loved serving our great country. Military women who trusted the system to protect them, and when it didn't, these same military women found a way to *carry on.*

They continued to serve honorably and mustered up the courage to move from victim to victor in their individual situations. They went from suffering in silence to finding their voice, telling their truth, and regaining their power. They chose to remain *silent no more!*

It is our hope that this healing chapter speaks to the warrior inside of you whose voice has been silenced.

May she find the strength to search out her own truth, the inspiration to raise her voice, and the encouragement to know that she is not alone or the only one.

Your healing awaits.

12

You Are Worth Protecting

Alice Gallop West

Trauma

Upon meeting me, many people find it hard to believe that I served in the military. For many, it takes a few seconds for them to digest. For others, they normally will look me squarely in the eye and ask, "How did you like being in the military?"

Without a moment's hesitation, I say, "The military was the best thing that I could have ever done."

That normally prompts other questions, and there ensues the conversation about my military career. Although my entry into the army was well over thirty years ago, there is so much of my life entwined with that single step of raising my right hand and taking the Oath of Enlistment on that unassuming early summer day in 1985.

As much as I knew what I was doing, I had no earthly idea what I was doing. Back then, I was pretty naïve and green to life. I had dreamed of going off to exotic places, living my life with newfound friends and a boundless energy to see the world beyond the life I was living in the quiet suburbs of northeast Baltimore.

Much like everyone before me, moving from being a citizen to a Soldier was quite uneventful. But all of that changed about six weeks into Basic Training, when I received word that my father had died unexpectedly at the young age of forty-two. I had spent hours training that day, so I was aware of the sweltering heat on that hellaciously hot, sunny day in July. He'd suffered a massive heart attack. Nothing could have prepared me for the news. When the words came out of my Drill Sergeant's mouth, I dropped my weapon. My battle buddy was by my side. As I sank to the ground crying, sobbing, breaking, somebody grabbed my rucksack off of my shoulders.

The chaplain asked me, "Do you want to go home?" That was a given. Not once did I ever think that I wouldn't go home. All I could think about was that my daddy was gone! My dad was my support system, my listening ear, my trusted confidant. He was my world. I had seen others leave in the middle of training. I knew that the life

I had created with my newfound friends and band of sisters in that old WWII barracks building we called home would change. I don't even remember packing to leave, but I know they helped. My battle buddy and my band of sisters put my things together in the same suitcase I arrived with.

Death is never easy, and for me, the death of my father was by far one of the most traumatic life events.

Divine Intervention

Returning to the unit following my father's funeral was difficult. I arrived the week my unit was in the field. I spent most of the first night just trying to figure out how much my life had changed as a result of my traumatic event. Early the next morning, I heard my platoon before I saw them—the excitement of returning from the field exercise could be heard throughout the halls. As much as everyone was glad to see me, I knew I would be leaving them soon to go to another training unit to complete Basic Training.

I was being "restarted." That dreaded term that meant I had to go back and start training from where I had left off. I was thankful that my unit made the process for me to move into a new unit smooth and easy. My Senior Drill Sergeant escorted me to the new unit. He even explained to the First Sergeant (1SG) why I was being restarted. He stated that I was one of the best Soldiers in the platoon, and if it had not been for my father's untimely death, and my having to leave to attend to his affairs, I would definitely be graduating with my unit.

I went on to graduate Basic Training with a new group of sisters. Although so much changed for me with my father's death, it was a welcome relief to know that I was always surrounded by new friends who showed so much care and concern for me. I know it was the love and support of my band of sisters who helped me make it through Basic Training, grief-stricken and hurting. I cried myself to sleep many nights. My new battle buddy said to me, "Why don't you go talk to the chaplain? It is okay to cry, but sometimes you need to talk things out." I was genuinely afraid to talk to the chaplain or anyone about how I was feeling and what I was going through.

Grief can be ugly at times.

I wasn't friendly anymore. I just wanted to finish my time and move on to my next duty station. I wanted to get away from Fort McClellan. I was beginning to not like where I was in life. As a result of being a restart, I ended up stuck at Fort McClellan much longer than expected, as a holdover awaiting orders for Advanced Individual Training (AIT). I often felt so alone even when I was in a room full of people. I asked the chaplain one Sunday after church if I could make an appointment to see him. I figured it definitely couldn't make matters any worse. Little did I know that one appointment would change the course of my entire military career.

The chaplain asked me if I could assist him at the chapel during the day instead of just sitting in the barracks cleaning or doing special details. This request lifted my spirits a little. I would have the opportunity to have a real day job. For nearly six months, every day and even on Sundays, I would walk over to the orderly room to sign out and then walk the short distance to the chapel to work. I did everything the chaplain assistants did. I answered the phones, made appointments, and typed up bulletins and programs for the chapel.

Many months passed, and due to a glitch with my AIT, I was offered the opportunity to change my military occupational specialty (MOS) to become a chaplain's assistant. Can you say divine intervention? After my on-the-job training, this decision was not a hard one to make. I jumped at the chance. The right people were in place to make the change happen quickly for me once everyone knew that I wanted to change my MOS. Before leaving Fort McClellan, I received my first award—an Army Achievement Medal—and I wasn't even MOS qualified, but I was well on my way.

From Trauma to Purpose

Being a chaplain's assistant for more than seven years in the US Army in many ways prepared me for working with victims of military crimes. Had the death of my father not occurred, I would not have been put in a position to meet the one person who forged a new chapter in my life, my unit chaplain. Granted, I would have preferred my father live to a ripe old age, but in the midst of my mourning and sorrow, something good was able to come of this situation. I believe God has a purpose for our lives, and everything we survive on the journey to our purpose is a necessary part of our story.

Later, I transitioned from the military and went to work at the Department of Army Civilians. I became one of the first civilian victim witness coordinators assigned to a military correctional facility. My sole purpose was to provide information and assistance to victims of military crimes. Many people are unaware how the life of a victim of military crimes is forever changed. Even those who are closest to victims or witnesses often do not understand how severely the trauma has impacted their lives. Many victims don't even comprehend how their own lives have been altered. Months and years can go by, and many crime victims and witnesses continue to suffer emotional pain and physical trauma. The truth is, becoming a victim or witness of a crime is not like wearing a badge of honor.

This unique community hides in plain sight as they work to understand the magnitude of their situation, conceal their true identity, and hope for a sense of normalcy as they rebuild their life in the aftermath.

For many of the years working in the victim advocacy field, I focused on educating our military community about the rights of victims and witnesses, as well as providing direct support to victims and witnesses of military crimes after an offender was sentenced to confinement. I would modestly say that I have assisted with hundreds of client cases during my tenure as a victim/witness coordinator for both army and navy. I would go as far to say that I was able to turn my trauma into my life's purpose. I feel so honored to serve this silent community of victims and witnesses, their lives tragically altered as a result of life circumstances. I've seen a lot over the years, from abductions, sexual assaults, spouse and child abuse, to homicide of a spouse or child at the hands of a service member.

Victims' rights are nothing new to the civilian community, but I found they were foreign to much of the military community I served. Unless you become a victim or know a victim, many people, even in leadership, are not aware of these rights in great detail. There has been a stigma in the military of those who reach out for help or even acknowledge that they are receiving help, especially if you are a victim or witness. More importantly, the rise in reporting military sexual trauma (MST) incidents lends itself to conclude that more offenders are being prosecuted and serving jail time for offenses that, in earlier years, would have gone unnoticed. As I write this, it still amazes me that few people know that the Military Victims Bill of Rights exists.

Military Victims Bill of Rights
1. *Be treated with fairness and respect for the victim's dignity and privacy.*
2. *Be reasonably protected from the accused offender.*
3. *Be notified of court proceedings.*
4. *Be present at all public court proceedings related to the offense, unless the court determines that testimony by the victim would be materially affected if the victim heard other testimony at trial.*
5. *Confer with the attorney for the government in the case.*
6. *Receive available restitution.*
7. *Be provided information about the conviction, sentencing, imprisonment, and release of the offender.*

Victims and witnesses of military crimes are all around us. We just don't talk about "such things." I have often said that the victim and witness community is a silent public relations program for the military services. Mothers and fathers have watched their children go off to war, and with the perils of war, there is a level of expectation that something could happen. That something normally makes the front page of a newspaper: Straight from the headlines, "Sergeant found stabbed," or "Fort XYZ Soldier was assaulted and left to die." In reality, the unnamed Sergeant or Soldier was a member of a family with parents, siblings, cousins, and a host of friends and military comrades. These parents, family members, and comrades of military service men and women are not adequately prepared to understand the maze of documents and procedures that come with being victims and witnesses. How the military treats this silent community of mothers, fathers, family members, and comrades during this difficult period of their lives speaks volumes about how the military community cares for its vulnerable.

Across the service branches, great strides have been taken to ensure that victims and witnesses of military crimes understand that they are not alone, and there are agencies and services to assist them. In the last fifteen years, program management and services to victims and witnesses have evolved into concentrated efforts to assist victims and witnesses from the moment a crime occurs, all the way through the incarceration process of an offender and beyond. Specific programs, such as Transitional Compensation, are available to family members whose service member is separated and/or incarcerated due to dependent related abuse. Transitional Compensation is a program designed to help families regain their dignity and reclaim their lives through a transitional process of financial and military service support.

Although so much has changed throughout the years, the rights afforded victims and witnesses have not changed. They remain constant to ensure that the military community provides the help and assistance that victims and witnesses so desperately need in their time of crisis. While my story does not include being a victim or witness to a military crime, I do understand living through traumatic life events. I've lived with the impact of losing my dad so young, and his absence has affected me throughout the course of my life. I understand how trauma can significantly alter one's life, and I bring this understanding and compassion to my job as a victims and witness coordinator (VWC).

If you find yourself in a situation where you are identified as a victim or witness to a military crime, remember the

Military Victims' Bill of Rights. Know that there is a system in place to protect, help, and preserve your dignity throughout the process of investigation, legal litigation, and if applicable, incarceration of the service member offender. Utilize this program and these services to get the help you need, mend a wrong, bridge the gap, and set the stage for healing to take place. That's why it is there.

So many of the stories in this book speak on the failures of the military system and how it has impacted the lives of victims and witnesses. These are not CSI stories written for television ratings; my Camouflaged Sisters in this book have *put pen to paper* and written real stories of the horrendous traumas they faced. It is important to remember that crime victims and witnesses have rights! Regardless of whether you are a military service member or a civilian. It is important that if you or someone you know is a victim or witness of a crime that they understand those rights. It is important that you have communication through a liaison appointed over your case to assist you in understanding those rights. Lastly, if the opportunity presents itself, it is important to know them at a sentencing hearing or even as a matter of parole and or clemency hearing.

Every victim and witness should ensure that they have a Victim Impact Statement on file with the court or parole agency. If the offender is sentenced many times, your Victim Impact Statement is read prior to the jury deliberation the judge's pronouncement of the sentence. Many times, this statement is read aloud by a family member or the victim, if applicable. If the offender is afforded a parole opportunity or a clemency hearing, ensure that the Victim Impact Statement is a part of the parole and clemency file. This ensures that those individuals who make decisions about sentencing, parole, and clemency matters understand the victim and witness, and how the crime has impacted not only the lives of the victim and or witness but also the lives of those around them.

13

You Are Worthy of Healing

Below are questions and answers that provide a little more insight on the healing process. Some of the authors offer suggestions for improvements to the system that are supposed to protect military women but don't always do a great job of that, while others share resources and services they used to help in their healing process. We hope these questions and answers help you in your own healing journey.

Can you provide some tips for someone seeking to develop a healthy spiritual life?

Lakisha Cole: As a woman who is also working on growing closer to God, there are a few tips that I would love to share:

1. Before anything else in your life (husband, marriage, children), always remember that God is first. If you have your own personal relationship with God, that will help you keep everything else in your life in order.

2. Always work to improve your relationship with Him. You should walk, talk, and look like a child of God. The first thing I do when I wake up is pray, thanking God for allowing me to see another day. I understand that it is a privilege to wake up every morning, and I take it as God's way of telling me that I'm on the journey to fulfill my life's purpose.

3. Take some time to meditate. This is also a great way to start your day. Meditation is a way to figure out what God's purpose is for your life. Everyone has a purpose, and you really have to search to find yours.

4. Become a part of the ministry teams at your local church.

5. Last but not least, be sure to tithe. Some people tend to think they pay their tithes every month, but you pay bills. You give tithes! Everything God has loaned you throughout your lifetime is simply that: a loan. You give tithes because you are giving back what God has already given unto you.

What has been the greatest factor in your life that allowed you to keep pushing forward despite life's challenges?

Karen Wright-Chisolm: I attribute all my success to God's grace. I believe I was to learn many lessons from my life's experiences, the number one lesson being that God has a purpose for my life. No matter what I had to go through to get to this point in my life, I know that God brought me through all of the obstacles I endured in my life for a reason. I believe that everything that happens in our lives happens for a reason.

I learned that the struggle is not just mine—many women, just like me, share this struggle. I've had many opportunities to help others, ultimately helping myself in my healing process. Being able to tell my story to others has motivated them to go on. While helping others, I have come to realize that my struggles were sometimes minimal compared to what someone else has gone through. Each time I mentored or nurtured others, their strength has helped me to heal over and over again. We feed off each other's strengths.

Another significant lesson I learned is that God brings us through struggles to teach us how to endure and how to pray. If we never experience any struggles, we will never know how to pray and what to pray for. The battle is not mine; the battle belongs to God.

How important is communication, and how does one find their voice in the midst of pain?

Ivy Edwards: Communication is extremely important in painful situations. Communication helps you understand the pain. Understanding is half the battle, which leads to the other half: management. It's hard to manage what we don't see, mental pain. Being able to communicate it in a way that gives it physical characteristics allows others to figure out how to help you. The doctor has a pain scale when you are in physical pain. He asks you to rate it, so he knows how to treat it.

When I was going through my struggle, I felt my pain growing inside of me and became very afraid of what I would birth. During natural childbirth, I was repeatedly told to breathe. I had to trust the process. This was a natural experience. When I got out of my own way (panicking and letting the pain take over), unbelievably, the pain was manageable and did not last as long. There's a thin line between controlling the pain and being controlled by the pain. Our body's reaction to stress often leads to physical ailments that become uncontrollable. Just remember to *breathe!*

Communicating that you are experiencing emotional pain can make you feel vulnerable and like a victim. Just know that you become victorious when you talk about it and work through it. We give words power by how we treat them. We often hold onto them like prized possessions—we don't want to share. When burden is shared, it is not as heavy. We have to change our perspective and have a willingness to let go. We have to trust the process. Release the words and thoughts into the universe to share with the world and take back your power! When you do this, you release other areas of your life from that painful, negative place as well. Open the doorway to those unhappy memories, give them a grieving period, and let them be comforted so they can rest in peace. That's real freedom, and freedom is life saving!

How important is it to embrace your authentic self in the healing process?

Lila Holley: Serving in the military changed me significantly. We are definitely changed, men and women alike, as a result of serving. In most cases, this is a change for the better. We become leaders, planners, team players, motivators, and so much more. These were the traits that allowed me to be successful and make it through a military career—traits that never leave me. I wanted my family and friends to focus on these traits that I excelled in while in the military.

In some cases, the change is not so good. Those of us who have been to combat or experienced trauma during our military career bear the hidden scars of those experiences. I wanted credit for taking steps to heal from the damage of those experiences. As a result, I learned to manage the negative effects of those experiences. I also learned to better communicate, which led to the discovery of my authentic self. I embraced all that I experienced in the military because it made me who I am today, and I happen to like her!

When I learned to like and love myself, I was able to fully embrace my authentic self unapologetically. As I embraced this newfound freedom, I was able to communicate more effectively, and I made my wellbeing a priority—again, unapologetically. I served a long time and gave freely to others before caring for myself, so making myself a priority was new to me. But you know what, it felt good; it felt right! I became a better version of myself, and in turn, I was able to better care for myself and those I love because I was able to create a healthy balance without forsaking my needs.

For many in the military, asking for help and going to counseling is a new experience, with many Veterans hesitant to seek out mental health services in their time of need. How has counseling helped

you deal with depression? What tips have you learned through counseling that help you manage bouts of depression?

Teresa Robinson: Counseling has been an ongoing process that helps me deal with depression and anxiety. At first, I was embarrassed to say that I needed help because I felt that I would be frowned upon as a noncommissioned officer (NCO) and leader. I felt it would be seen as a sign of weakness. But once I was able to find a counselor who I felt comfortable with, my healing process started, which meant more to me than being embarrassed. The counselor had to be someone who would listen to me and someone who I felt comfortable talking with.

Although it is an ongoing process for me, I recognize my trigger points. I found that the depression occurs October through April and during special days. In addition, the anxiety occurs during the loss of a loved one or friend. So what I try to do is keep busy by participating in my favorite hobbies: sewing and event planning. Talking to a counselor has allowed me to talk openly about my experiences, hurt, and pain without being judged.

Some of the tips I have learned through counseling that help me manage my bouts of depression are:

1. Don't be embarrassed to seek help.
2. Keep a daily journal of your feelings related to what causes the depression.
3. Be able to recognize your triggers for the depression and try to deflect your emotions and behavior.
4. Write a list of the special memories you have with your loved one.
5. Don't go to the gravesite every day. If you believe there is a Higher Being and that your loved one is there spiritually, then don't dwell on the death but the special memories.
6. Take medications as prescribed.
7. Stay mentally and physically active.
8. Have a good support system.

Many MST victims have many reasons for not reporting incidents, to include perceived flaws with the reporting system, their truthfulness questioned, the stigma that follows, and the possible threat of retaliation. Do you feel that with the improvements made over time by DoD and the VA, with regard to MST reporting and services, the system is now more inviting for victims to report incidents and/or seek the help they need to heal?

Monique Jones: Improvements have been made in the reporting system because now victims of MST have the option to report in confidentiality to a DoD-certified sexual assault responder and victim advocate solely for medical help and counseling. A variety of hotlines have also been implemented, yet victims still have to be extremely careful who they tell and what they tell. Let's say I decide I want to tell a friend or trusted leader first. With that confession, I may have just lost the chance for that report to remain in the confidential reporting channel.

There is still a long way to go to create a flawless system. Many who suffer in silence remain uncomfortable about reporting in the military system. They question if the system is really set up to protect them and truly hold assailants accountable.

Then there is the issue of privacy and confidentiality as it pertains to accountability. How does someone go to appointments without being questioned as to their whereabouts? There are many implications for not being at your place of duty without an explanation. Perception is everything in the military. An MST survivor could be labeled a slacker just for seeking help.

My healing was important to me, and that is why I looked for help outside the military system I couldn't trust to fully protect and assist me. This choice assured me of total confidentiality, something that was important to me and critical in my healing. I was even willing to pay out of pocket for expenses because my peace of mind is priceless to me. I was able to establish rapport with my provider and make great strides in my healing.

My advice to anyone seeking counseling services is that you take the time to find the person you feel comfortable with. I liken it to finding that perfect pair of jeans: the fit has to be just right for survivors of MST. Your healing depends on treatment that is the right fit for you.

The first seventy-two hours are crucial following an MST attack. The capacity of a unit to properly respond to an incident can literally determine the speed and/or difficulty of a victim's recovery. What are the three most important pieces or steps of the Sexual Harassment Assault and Response Program (SHARP) that allows a unit to be properly positioned to respond to an MST incident?

Merci L. McKinley: In order for a unit to properly position itself to respond to a report of sexual assault, they must make sure that the standard operating procedures (SOPs) are in place. The SOPs should address every aspect, including

- the report
- the immediate response

- the treatment of the future survivor
- compliance with investigative procedures
- streamline of support and care for the survivor throughout the entire process according to the type of report made

The unit must ensure the first responder and/or SHARP victim advocate is properly trained, and the proper credentials are kept up to date and in accordance with applicable regulations.

Part of this process is making sure that the victim advocate has response packets readily available and response kits properly stocked and easily accessible at a moment's notice. It is vital that the unit remain unbiased but take swift and immediate action that is conducive to the health and welfare of the future survivor. Often in the military, we are accustomed to being reactive, but being reactive is not necessarily beneficial in addressing a report of MST. It is imperative that a unit becomes proactive with SHARP because the first seventy-two hours are the most critical for collecting evidence, going through the chain of custody, and addressing the immediate reaction of the survivor as he or she begins to process what has occurred.

Physical ailments often go overlooked as being directly related to one's traumatic experience. Can you share how you were able to tie the two together, and what should others look for to properly make the connection within themselves?

Cleve Williams: I experienced headaches, chest pains, heart palpitations, rapid breathing, hyperventilation, hair loss, numbness in my arm, and occasional numbness in my legs. These symptoms were followed by dizziness, blackouts, insomnia, fatigue, and nausea some years later.

I had nightmares, which helped me link the panic attacks to the trauma, and I linked most of the other symptoms through the process of elimination. After ruling out every other possibility through doctor's visits and talking about how and when I experienced them is how I was able to tie them together. The key is to communicate with your doctor and be active in your treatment plan to find answers—to identify *your truth*. Your total wellbeing requires that you are honest in your communication and that you actively participate in executing your treatment plan.

How has speaking and sharing your story helped you in your healing process?

Rajsheda Griffin: Experiencing domestic violence in my first real relationship was traumatizing for me, and it seriously messed up my views on relationships. I always asked God, why me? I never received an answer until the day that I did my first speaking engagement. Speaking in front of others about my experience was extremely hard, but afterwards, I had so many women and men reach out to me and ask for assistance. They said because I shared my experience, it helped them to step up and get help. It was at that moment I realized that this experience happened to me not because of something I did, but because I was meant to share my story and help others.

Empathy is something that helps us feel how others feel and be able to put ourselves in others' shoes. Since I have been through this domestic violence experience, I can empathize with other females. I know the pain, hurt, and trials they face. None of it is easy—surviving the abuse, leaving the abuser, or seeking support. When women are in an abusive relationship, they sometimes feel alone and that there is no one to turn to. When I speak to audiences, there is a small percentage of women who have been abused or are in an abusive relationship (it has happened with nearly every audience I have spoken with). When they hear my testimony and experiences, they know they aren't alone. It is my hope that my words reach the hearts of victims and let them know that others have also experienced this, and if they can go from victim to victor, then there is hope for them in their situation. Healing is closer than you think. *You open up possibilities for healing when you share your story.*

About the Authors

Lila Holley

Lila Holley is a retired US Army Chief Warrant Officer Four and award-winning visionary author behind the Camouflaged Sisters brand. This two-time, #1 bestselling author is on a mission to empower military women to raise their voices and tell their stories. She has created multiple platforms and outlets for military women to share their stories with the world: the Camouflaged Sisters books; an online radio show, "In Session with the Camouflaged Sisters"; The Sisterhood, an online community where journaling and blogging are encouraged; plans to launch a biannual magazine for military women; and live events where military women will take center stage and share even more of their incredible stories.

Lila loves to relax by cooking and spending time with her loving family. Contact Lila at contactme@lilaholley.com or at her website http://lilaholley.com.

Rajsheda Griffin

Rajsheda Griffin joined the United States Army in 2003, about four years after graduation from Bruton High School in Williamsburg, Virginia. She is currently serving her eleventh year in the United States Army as an Automated Logistics Specialist. She is a single mother of three girls. Her hobbies include public speaking, praise dancing, weightlifting, and spoken word poetry.

Rajsheda is a domestic violence survivor. She shares her experience to encourage others that they do not deserve to be abused. She has spoken to over 1,000 individuals in seminars, military balls, and galas. Her goal is to reach out to individuals in the military as well as in the civilian sector to raise awareness of domestic violence and make sure more resources are available to victims. She also wishes to help aid survivors and help them rebuild themselves following an abusive relationship.

Vivian Palmer

Vivian Palmer was born and raised in New York, New York. She served in the Healthcare Corps during her seven years of military service, with one tour of duty in Frankfurt, Germany. With over twenty years in the medical field, Vivian continues to serve Veterans as a Nursing Supervisor at a State Veterans Home in Central Texas.

Vivian has been an avid athlete all her life. In 2015, she became the first African American woman and Veteran to own a professional men's basketball team in the American Basketball Association (ABA) in Central Texas. Learn more at www.texasskyriders.com

Karen Wright-Chisolm

Karen Wright-Chisolm served in USAF for twenty-seven years. Karen is the first female and first African American to hold the position of Superintendent, 315th Mission Support Squadron, Charleston, South Carolina.

Karen is a Doctoral of Management Candidate, Organizational Leadership. She holds a dual MA degree in HR management/development from Webster University; a BS degree in HR management from Southern Wesleyan University; and an AA degree in HR management/ personnel administration from CCAF.

Karen is a Life Member of Tuskegee Airmen, Air Force Sergeants Association, and Board Member of Boots 2 Heels, Inc. She is married to Paul Chisolm Jr. and has four children, Tamara, Eric, Paul III, and Jazmine.

Merci L. McKinley

Merci L. McKinley is a Veteran of the US Army, serving thirteen years before being medically retired as a Staff Sergeant. She currently serves as an independent contractor in support of the DoD. Merci has received numerous accolades during her service, but her greatest reward is her duty as a sexual harassment assault response and prevention victim advocate.

Merci enjoys speaking to bring awareness to the issues of military sexual trauma and domestic violence, and she works to assist victims of military sexual trauma grow from victim to survivor. She also assists Veterans and their families as they transition from military service. Merci is now working to start a non-profit organization. She is a native of Prince George's County, Maryland.

Cleve Williams

Cleve Williams is a Veteran of the U.S. Army, where she honorably served for six years. Cleve is a mother and is the only daughter of four children. She describes herself as a freelance creative stylist. Cleve believes that her experiences and the fact that she was raised in a military family gives her a greater appreciation for the sacrifices made by military personnel and their families. Contact Cleve at cwilliv2r@gmail.com.

Monique Jones

Monique "mojo" Jones is a dynamic and energetic speaker who speaks and helps others into finding their personal MOJO after trauma! Her focus is on the importance of having resilience and courage in the face of life's adversities, such as sexual trauma. She uses her sixteen years of active duty military and personal experiences to empower and inspire people worldwide. She is an honored member of the International Society of Business Leaders for her twenty plus years of work in the healthcare industry. She also serves as a World Vision Humanitarian and Child Advocate who promotes quality of life for children worldwide. For more information or booking info, contact mojo2speak@gmail.com.

Michelle Dowleyne

Michelle Dowleyne was born in Columbus, Georgia, and raised in Detroit, Michigan. She entered into the United States Army in 1989 and served twenty-two years faithfully. She is the founder and CEO of Boots 2 Heels, Inc., a nonprofit that assists female Veterans to transform their lives back to the civilian world.

Michelle is a motivational speaker for women empowerment and military issues. She is the best-selling author in the anthology Empowered Women of Social Media, in which forty-four women found their voices using the power of social networking. She is also a contributing author in the anthology D.I.V.A.S. - Driven Individual Visionaries Accomplish Success: How 12 Women Turned their MESSage into a MOVEMENT

Teresa Robinson

Teresa Robinson is a retired US Army Veteran who served honorably for over twenty-one years. She is currently employed with the Department of Defense as a certified medical laboratory technician. She holds a bachelor's degree from the University of Mary-Hardin Baylor. Teresa is very active in the community and belongs to numerous organizations, including Women Army Corps Veterans' Association, American Medical Technology (AMT), and National Healthcare Association.

Teresa loves traveling and spending time with her family, her husband who is also a UA Army Veteran, and her two children. Teresa recently started a business, Pearl Girlz Support All Cancers, to bring awareness to all form of cancers and support those who have been affected by this deadly disease.

Ivy Edwards

Ivy Edwards is married with two sons, aged twenty-five and thirteen. She was only twenty years old when she was activated in support of Operation Desert Storm. The war actually ended on her twenty-first birthday, February 28, 1991. She resides in Chesterfield, Virginia, and enjoys cooking, reading, writing, and learning life's lessons. She shows love through her food and on any given Sunday, you can find family gathered at her kitchen table.

Ivy admits she "camouflaged" herself for years and only recently opened up about a traumatic experience during Desert Storm. She describes herself as a work in progress and focuses on being more open and honest in her communications as she seeks to find the true gems in this world. She vows to surround herself with positive people, take no one for granted, and let the death of her friend, Pamela Gay, not be in vain.

Lakisha Coles

Baltimore native Lakisha Coles currently resides in Killeen, Texas, as a Retired US Army Chief Warrant Officer Two with seventeen years of active federal service. She deployed in support of Operation Iraqi Freedom (one tour) and Operation Enduring Freedom (three tours).

With an associates of arts degree from Fayetteville Technical Community College and a bachelors of arts degree in criminal justice from Ashford University, Lakisha now enjoys life as an entrepreneur.

Lakisha believes that God is the reason for all her success and accomplishments and aspires to grow closer to Him. Her goals are to motivate, inspire, and encourage others to be the best that God wants them to be. To learn more, visit www.therealkishacoles.com

Alice Gallop West

West is a native of Baltimore, Maryland. She holds a bachelor's of science degree in social work (BSSW) from Spalding University. She is a graduate of the Department of Army, Army Management Staff College. Alice holds several certificates and has completed advanced graduate course work from the University of Kentucky School of Social Work and Comprehensive Victim Intervention Specialist (Intermediate) Credentialed Advocate. In 2004, she was recognized by the American Corrections Association (ACA) and DoD as being the Best of the Best in Army corrections.

Alice has garnered more than twenty-eight years of active federal service, beginning with her career in the US Army, which began in June 1985.

SHARE YOUR THOUGHTS

With the Author: If this book has impacted you in any way, the author would be delighted to hear about it. Send an email to *author@publishyourgift.com.*

Looking for a Speaker? Book the author to speak at your next event by writing to *booking@publishyourgift.com.*

Discover great books, exclusive offers, and more at
www.PublishYourGift.com

Connect with us on social media

@publishyourgift